# Hero Habits

*THRIVING*

The Guide to ~~Surviving~~ in
Corporate America *+ IN LIFE*

*Arnie,
You Are A Real Life
Super Hero!!!*

*Hahndo* ☺

# MICHAEL H. HAHN

*Beyond...*
GOOD TEAMS

Published by

BEYOND GOOD TEAMS, LLC
Lisle, IL 60532

The Hero and Villain character distinctions were developed in partnership and with permission by PREP Profile Systems, Inc. I gratefully acknowledge the references and direct quotes to personality, which are reprinted with express permission from PREP Profile Systems, Inc., of which I am a master certified facilitator and administrator. Unauthorized distribution without permission from PREP is prohibited. For further information about PREP and their extensive product validation, visit www.prep-profiles.com

Special discounts are available for bulk purchases to use for sales promotions, employee premiums, or educational purposes. Please e-mail **Info@HeroHabits.org** for more information and to order.

Cover designed by Justinstrode.com

Printed in the United States of America

Library of Congress Cataloging-in-Publication Data is available.

**ISBN: 978-0692874790**

To my amazing wife,
for her endless hours of devotion, ongoing
support, and honest feedback. I couldn't have
completed this without you!

# Table of Contents

# Prologue

Hi, I'm James, and I'm embarrassed by what you're about to read. When I look back, it's easy to see what was happening. I should have seen it coming, but I didn't…

This is my story. Take it easy on me, OK?

Two weeks ago, I was caught up in the swirl, putting in long hours and getting limited sleep. I was pushing too hard, making poor decisions, and struggling to be present with my family. I was slipping from being the hero to being the villain.

Little things started to really bother me. My daily battle with traffic, the endless days of meetings, and all the diverse personalities at work were driving me nuts. In short, my life was slipping away, and I didn't know that a perfect storm of unexpected challenges was about to bring me to my knees.

In my defense, I was busy trying to provide for my family and make a name for myself. I had recently been promoted and assigned a couple of challenging projects. I had taken on too much and was too proud to ask for help. I thought I was hiding my stress, but my family and friends were growing tired of watching me become someone else.

Ten days prior, Suzy and I took a well-deserved vacation to Mexico, where I struggled to shift out of work mode. Although I was able to salvage most of the vacation and reconnect with Suzy and our son, Mason, the relaxation quickly faded when the reality of reentry at work and the daily grind of our life started to sink in again.

We had just finished dinner and were about to have an argument about my attitude, our relationship, and Suzy's stress. Little did I know that a phone call was about to change my life forever…

MICHAEL HAHN

# ONE

# The Wake-Up Call
## The Day Life Turned Upside Down

James, did you fill out Mason's soccer registration?"
Suzy scraped Mason's dinner plate and spied James on his tablet. She tossed the plate in the dishwasher. "Did you even hear me?"

"Yeah, sure, Suzy. You asked if I filled something out, right?"

Spinning on her heels, Suzy placed the full weight of her attention upon James. "This is exactly what we talked about when we were on vacation. Even when you are physically here, you are mentally somewhere else!

"You promised that when we got back from vacation, life would be different. You promised that you would make us a priority, but we haven't even been back two weeks, and you are already putting us second to whatever it is you're looking at!"

"Look, Suzy, you're blowing this out of proportion. I'm just checking some field reports for a presentation Tuesday morning…"

James trailed off in midsentence, his eyes following Suzy's phone as it sputtered face down across the countertop.

"I'll get it for you." He reached toward her phone.

"James, leave it! There is absolutely nothing more important than this conversation. Just leave it alone!"

"OK, I won't get it then..."

"James, I'm exhausted. We push so hard every day, and it just feels like we are on different teams. You didn't even try to help prepare for our vacation."

"That's not true!"

"It is true! I booked the hotel, the airline, and the ride to the airport. I packed my bag and Mason's bag, and you were still packing when our ride showed up."

"Come on now. Quit blowing this out of proportion!"

"I'm not blowing it out of proportion. What were you doing, anyway? Let me guess: you were busy taking care of your family by neglecting us, right?"

James's eyelid started to twitch. "That hurts!"

Suzy sniffed back her tears. "You were checking e-mails on the way to the airport, in the terminal, and for the first two days of our vacation. I've been picking up the slack at home ever since you took that promotion!"

"*Honey*...it did take me a couple days to disconnect, but once I did, we had a ton of fun. We took Mason on his first Jet Ski ride, swam with the dolphins, and went zip-lining as a family. We even danced to the mariachis after dinner, remember? Just like the old days!"

"Why did it take you so long? You have a great family, a loving wife, and a good job, but nothing is ever good enough for you lately. I wish you'd never taken that stupid promotion anyway!"

"You know this job is how I provide for the family. I have a lot to absorb in my new role; it feels like the more I learn, the less I know. Besides—"

Suzy's phone buzzed again, but she didn't flinch. Her eyes were glassy with tears, frustration, and anger.

"I work too! I provide an income for the family. Then I pick up Mason from school and take him to his activities, and then I rush home to make sure you're all fed a healthy dinner. I do all of this, and you repay me by only listening half the time and grunting at me the other half. This isn't what you promised in our vows! This isn't what I signed up for!"

"But I—" James tried to interrupt Suzy's accusations.

"I planned the trip, not because you needed it, but because I needed it. I needed something to look forward to, so I could disconnect from my endless responsibilities. It's been less than two weeks, and I'm even more stressed than before we left. Don't you even care?"

"I do care! You and Mason are my top priority. I'm sorry; I'm still trying to figure out how to make this all work. I feel like I'm juggling everything and trying not to let anything drop."

"For the past year, you've been saying things would be different once you got this promotion. Now you are telling me you need more time. There is always going to be some excuse as to why you aren't present with us. If you keep waiting for everything to be perfect, you just might wake up alone one day."

*I'm such a failure!* James slumped down into the kitchen chair.

Suddenly, he felt his phone vibrate against his leg. Instinctually, he pulled it from his pocket and swiped his finger across the screen.

"Unbelievable!" Suzy shook her head and walked toward the stairs.

"Oh, hello, Sharon," James stuttered, a bit louder than normal.

Suzy slowed her departure as a chill ran up her spine. "Mom?"

"James, I need to talk to Suzy, but I keep getting her voice mail!

Is she there?"

"Sure, Sharon. She's right here…"

Suzy snatched the phone from his outstretched hand and tried to hold back her tears. "Hi, Mom. I'm kind of in the middle of—"

"Suzy, I've got bad news about your father."

"Bad news? What do you mean? Is Dad OK?"

"Honey…your father had a massive seizure this afternoon and left us…"

The phone slipped from Suzy's ear, and guilt consumed her. "Dad's gone? There must be some mistake…I've been so busy juggling everything, and now Dad…No, no, no, this isn't happening!"

Suzy wiped the tears streaming down her cheeks, and her mom continued.

"He left us for two minutes, but you know how stubborn your father is!"

"Wait, Mom. Is Dad alive?"

The seconds felt like hours as Suzy prayed for a second chance.

"Sorry, honey. You know your father wouldn't give up that easily."

Suzy wiped her eyes, sniffed repeatedly, and started crying all over again.

"He has been in out of consciousness all afternoon. He awoke for a few moments and said, 'I saw this incredible white light. I just kept walking straight up to it until I stood at the pearly gates. I saw our sons smiling back at me. They said, "Pops, it's not your time. You still have work to do."'"

"Dad's alive? Where is he? How is he doing?"

"Well, the doctor said that he is lucky to be alive. He had a grand mal seizure and completely lost sight in his left eye. The field of vision in his right eye is the size of a straw."

"Oh, Mom, I need to see Dad! And you too."

"Suzy, I know you have a lot going on, but I think a visit from you might be the only thing he's clinging to right now. The doctor said your father is stable, but he has some severely blocked arteries that could trigger a heart attack, a stroke, or another seizure."

"I'll be on the first flight out in the morning. Promise you'll give him a huge hug and kiss from me." Suzy, clinging to her second chance, closed her eyes. "And tell him I love him, OK?"

After she hung up, Suzy fell into James's chest, instantly flooding him with memories.

*I remember when Bill taught me how to make fire with only flint and steel at Camp Thunderbird. My first visit to the comic book store… the day he let me drive his '69 Stingray…and at our college graduation, when he gave me permission to marry my high-school sweetheart. Poor Suzy. Her heart must be breaking…*

"I'm sorry about Dad," James said. "I'm here for you. I love you!"

Suzy began pounding James's chest, trying to wake up from her nightmare. He held her close, slowly stroking her platinum-blond hair.

"James, I *need* to go. Dad has always been there for me, and he needs me more than ever. I know we have a lot going on, but I know you can find a way to make it work. You always do!"

Suzy marched up the stairs, wiping her face as tears rolled down her cheeks. Her mind spun wildly with the logistics required for her trip: tickets, packing, coverage for her work projects and Mason's activities.

*How's this going to work?* James wondered. *I know she has a lot going on right now, but so do I. I can't believe Bill almost died! I thought he would be around forever…well, at least long enough to see Mason grow up, get married, and have kids. Suzy must be in shock. I know she's just trying to process this, and I'm on the receiving end of it. I seem to be there a lot more lately…*

**TWO**

# The Reality Check
## Meet Doctor Doubtful

*really want to be here for Suzy, but I need to prepare for my client meeting with Chris Raven,* James thought. *This could be my big break. I need to prove myself; otherwise I might not be able to keep us in this house. I don't want to force Mason to leave his school and his friends. Why does this keep happening to me?*

After a rough night with Suzy and a less-than-stellar early-morning departure at the airport, James rushed Mason to school and then bolted into work. A lengthy gapers' delay tested his already limited patience and fueled his growing frustration.

*There just isn't enough time in the day. Why now? Why me? Why can't life just be simple again? Suzy's upset with me, and I don't get to spend much time with Mason. I feel like I'm losing control!*

After arriving at work, James went head down, working diligently for an extended burst interrupted only by thoughts of Suzy and Bill.

*I wonder how Suzy is feeling. She must have arrived by now. I wish I could help her. I wish I could just make this all better!*

The morning flew by until the grumble in his belly and the smell of hot pizza lured him away from his desk.

*Is that*—he sniffed—*Giordano's pizza? It sure is! I'll just zap these two last pieces—and jackpot, a cookie! All right, if I can keep hammering my to-do list for the rest of the afternoon, that might allow a little time to dive into the historical reports to better prepare for my client meeting tomorrow.*

James's feeling of accomplishment faded when a reminder flashed on his phone.

Pick up Mason from school. Leave by 5:00 p.m.

*Where did the day go?* James began clicking through the drop-down menus.

*All right, I'll save my files, set my out-of-office message, and pack my bag. Do I have my phone, wallet, and keys? Check, check, and check!*

James bolted down the stairs and across the parking lot. For the next thirty-five minutes, he followed the endless stream of brake lights and mentally added to his never-ending to-do list. Then he shook his head in disbelief and pounded his fists on the steering wheel.

*Come on…seriously? Can traffic get any worse? Let's go, people!*

After another ten minutes, he turned into the school parking lot and dashed to the gym to pick up Mason from soccer practice.

James's and Mason's eyes met. "There's my boy!"

"Dad!"

"Hey, bud. How was school today?"

"It was all right, Dad. Can you carry my backpack?"

"Sure, bud, no problem." James grabbed it from him. "You can carry this all by yourself? You must be getting pretty strong."

"I sure am! It's part of my superhero training."

James savored the moment, ruffling Mason's hair.

"Are we going to the trampoline park?" Mason asked.

James nodded as his phone shook with another reminder.

Annual Exam/Blood Test Results: Leave by 5:45 p.m.

James looked up to see Mason's toothy grin.

"Uh, sorry, bud, not tonight. I promised Mom I'd go the doctor."

"Come on, Dad. I want to go to the trampolines. How can I ever become a superhero if I don't practice? Hmm, I've got it! We can do it *together!*"

James engaged in a long, slow blink, attempting to process Mason's request.

"Listen, bud, you can't always get what you want! You'll just have to wait."

"Wait for what?" Mason protested.

"This isn't what I want, little man. I need to follow through on my commitment to your mother."

James remembered his all too recent conversation with Suzy when he argued about not having enough time to review the lab results and Suzy's retort that she did not want any more health surprises. He pulled into the doctor's parking lot and dragged himself from the car while Mason unbuckled his booster seat.

*Gray and overcast...perfect mood lighting for my doctor's visit. Lately, I'm the one who's always raining on Mason's parade. After this visit, maybe I can squeeze in some fun time for him while I review the site-comparison files.*

"Listen, bud, if you are a good boy while we are with the doctor, maybe we can grab dinner from a special place, OK?"

Mason scuffed his feet across the asphalt, still engaging in his quiet revolt.

After following the standard doctor's office protocol, James slipped off his scuffed black dress shoes and stepped on the scale.

"204 pounds. OK, now turn around so I can get your height."

"Wait, what? That can't be right. I'm only 184 pounds."

"Sorry, James, the scale doesn't lie. Follow me." The nurse continued making notes in her tablet until she opened the door to one of the many patient rooms.

"Go ahead and take a seat. The doctor will see you in a few minutes."

James looked at Mason. "OK, bud, while I'm talking to the doctor, I want you to make some progress on your homework, all right?"

"But, Dad, this isn't how it works. I've been in school all day! Mom always lets me have a snack and watch a show before I do my homework."

"Mason, things are going to be different while Mom is gone."

Mason huffed for a moment until a knock interrupted them and the door swung open.

"Hi, James. I'm Dr. Leah. Dr. Collins is on maternity leave, and I'm covering for her while she's out."

*Wow, I didn't know Dr. Collins was even trying to get pregnant...*

"Have a seat." The doctor patted the empty seat next to her.

Scanning over the report, she said, "I see it's been a while since you've last visited with us. James, you know, we need to see you at least once a year."

"It's been just over a year," James stammered defensively. His tone caused Mason to slowly lift his eyes from his book.

"No, James, it's been almost three years since you were here, and I see some fairly obvious signs that we need to address. You've gained

20 pounds, and your cholesterol is 226. Your good cholesterol is too low, your bad cholesterol is too high, and your blood pressure is nearly high risk."

James shrank in his seat like a scolded schoolboy. He tried to push his seat farther from the doctor, looking to regain some personal space.

*Twenty pounds heavier? Well, my pants have been kinda tight...*

"Let's review your eating habits, James. Our records show that you were eating salad three days per week and a half sandwich and soup the other days. I'm just curious, James. What did you eat for lunch today?"

"Uh, today?"

James mind flashed to the two pieces of Giordano's pizza and the chocolate-chip cookie he had devoured on his way back from the work kitchen.

"Today was an anomaly..."

The doctor looked up from her report.

"An anomaly, James? Your cholesterol doesn't get to be 226 from eating half sandwiches, salads, and soups."

James started to squirm under the doctor's not-so-subtle interrogation.

"Let's review your weekly activity. It says here that you were doing 30 minutes of cardio at the gym three times per week and attending karate for two hours per week. Is that still correct?"

"Kinda. I get to the gym when I can, but I haven't been doing that routine since I had surgery."

"When was that?"

"Last May. No, wait. It was the year before..."

Then the realization hit. His excuses had been mounting since he'd ruptured his ACL almost three years before.

"James, when was the last time you went to karate or the gym?"

James shifted his eyes to the ceiling as he thought.

"Well, I worked out once while we were in Mexico, and since we retuned, I've just been so busy, and now that Suzy's gone…"

The doctor entered James's responses into her tablet.

"James, how would you rate your stress on a scale of one to ten, with one meaning no stress to ten meaning totally stressed?"

*My stress level? I've got so much to do and so little time. Everybody wants something from me, and it feels like I just can't get caught up. I'm constantly running from one thing to the next and don't have a moment to myself. I feel bad taking time from my family to go to the gym, and I'm torn because I know I'm thinking about other things when I'm with them. My life is so demanding! Lately it feels like I just can't win…*

Breaking the silence, the doctor said, "James, give me a number."

"9.5" James sank under the weight of his confession.

*I used to be invincible. What's happened to me?*

"James, I can tell you what you need to do, but it's up to you to make it happen." The doctor paused. "What do you love to do that you just don't have time for anymore?"

"Karate…I loved karate. I mean I love karate."

James thoughts drifted back to their Hawaiian honeymoon, when he and Suzy had practiced their karate forms on the gritty sand beaches of Hanalei Bay.

"Karate has always been a physical, mental, and spiritual exercise for me. Before my knee injury, life was easy! Now it's about making everyone else happy." *Or at least trying not to make them mad.*

"James, I've seen many people assume that as they age and have children, they will gain weight and become sluggish. They say it's just part of growing old. They tell me they work out all the time, but they can't remember the last time they went to the gym or even broke a sweat. They say they eat well, but they forget about eating pizza and cookies…Are you one of *those* people?"

The doctor paused, allowing the weight of the question to resonate.

"*No!* I'm not one of those people. Everything changed after my injury."

"Good. There are others who take this message and reconnect with old passions. They stop making *excuses*, and they start scheduling time to work out. They tell me that in just a few weeks, they're less stressed, they've dropped some weight, and they feel an energy boost. They tell me they've become better spouses, parents, and leaders. But the choice is up to you."

James pursed his lips and clenched his jaw.

*I'm trying my best! What doesn't she understand about that? She doesn't even know me, and she's treating me like one of those lifeless corporate zombies.*

"James, in six months, I want to do another blood panel so we can check your progress. If you're committed to working out and making better food choices, you could see tremendous results! What do you think?"

James, still fuming, nodded his head in agreement.

The doctor finished entering her notes and washed her hands. Before she left she leaned forward, invading James's personal space, and continued in a hushed tone.

"James, this won't work if you do this because I told you to do it. You need to do this because you want to live a long healthy life."

She handed James his paperwork. "Please give this to Lexy, and she can schedule your six-month follow-up appointment."

*I can't believe she gave me that lecture. I've been so good lately. I've stopped drinking soda and reduced my late-night snacking! It must be so easy to look at a printed report and make assumptions about what I have been doing and should be doing. That's irresponsible; I would never do that! And where is her bedside manner, anyway?*

"Grab your backpack, Mason. Let's go!"

Mason knew better than to say anything when Dad had that tone.

*Who does she think she is? Forget her. Forget this place! Replacement doctor, huh? She's more like a replacement scrub.*

"James, would you like to schedule your follow-up now?" Lexy's soft voice inquired from behind the counter as James plowed toward the exit.

"No thanks!"

He tore open the heavy wooden door and stomped out.

"Hurry up and get in," he told Mason.

James slammed his door and began muttering under his breath.

"I can't believe she had the gall to talk to me like that. I thought she was supposed to help people be healthy and highlight the positive health changes people are making. All she did was doubt me. She's *evil!*"

James squeezed the steering wheel and shook his head.

"Dad, she was not nice!"

"You're right, Mason. She shouldn't talk to people like that."

James slipped the SUV into reverse and headed toward the highway.

"Yeah, Dad. I think she's a villain!"

Mason's words reverberated in James's head.

*Villain? Yeah, villain…She has no idea what I've been going through these past six months—heck, these past three years. I thought she was supposed to find the good in people, but she's skeptical I'll make any changes.*

"You're right, Mace; she is a villain. She didn't look for the good things I am doing. She made a bunch of assumptions and cast her toxic judgment on me."

"Yeah, Dad, she is a *bad* finder, not a good finder!"

James started to think about Mason's words.

*She was suspicious, formal, and perfectionistic. She didn't see me as a person, just as some numbers on a stupid report. I mean, how hard would it be to look at the progress I've made and start by highlighting what is working?*

"Listen, Mason, she was a total faultfinder! She made a bunch of negative assumptions about me and is doubtful that I can fix it. She was only focused on what she wanted to believe."

"She's a doubtful doctor. That's it, I got it. She's Dr. Doubtful!"

"Doctor Doubtful? Hmm. Well, she was cold and distant. Her icy words cut right through me, and she didn't allow me to get past her frozen exterior." James glanced in the rearview mirror and noticed Mason clenching his fists and shadowboxing the headrest-mounted TV.

"Thank you, Mason! I know you're on my side, buddy."

*Uh-oh, I think I just crossed the line. Mason is taking on my frustration and bitterness. I hate it when I do that! How can I make this right? Oh, I know...*

"Are you hungry? I think we need to stop by Extreme Trampoline for some dinner and a little superhero training."

"Huh? That's *awesome*, Dad!"

*Doctor Doubtful*

# THREE

# Hero Training
Making Memories

James watched Mason bound from one trampoline to the next, heading toward the large foam pit at the end of the warehouse. "All right, Mason's happy. Now to check on Suzy…"
James tapped out a text.

Hi Suz…Just checking in. Are you at the hospital yet?

Then he flipped over to his work e-mail.
*Great! Luis sent the comparative reports for the southeast call center. Hmm, I wonder how they did last month with the spike in call volumes.*
"Dad…Dad…DAD!"
James's hearing faded as he searched for the hidden treasure buried deep within the reports.
"Dad, are you watching? Look, Dad! *Look!* I'm flying!"
When Mason didn't get an immediate response, his eyes dropped to his feet, and his smile faded to a pouty frown.
Then, finally, James looked at Mason.
"Nice work, son. You are *flying!*"

*I know Mason is in his element, and I should be paying more attention, but I just have so much riding on tomorrow's meeting!*

"Dad, watch this…"

Mason sprang off the final trampoline with his arms spread out to the sides and dove into the pit of brightly colored foam shapes.

"Super Mason…to the rescue!" James blurted.

Mason smiled, accepting his father's limited attention.

Then James's phone vibrated with Suzy's response.

> Sorry, the flight had a maintenance delay and my battery died. Mom just picked me up and we're on the way to the hospital. I'm sorry. I've been pretty stressed lately.

So glad you are safe and with Mom. Is she all right?

> Mom is great. I missed her so much! She says Dad should be awake when we arrive.
> You went to your doctor appointment, right?

Yeah, let's talk after you see Dad, OK?

> Sounds good. Give Mason a hug and kiss for me, Super Daddy.

I love you! (couple kissing emoji)

> I love you too!

*At least Suzy arrived safe and is feeling better. It's been tough trying to balance work and home…and recently it seems like I'm always off by just a few degrees!*

James pressed the home button and spotted the time.

*Oh shoot, we'd better get some food so we can get out of here.*

He scanned the faded menu board for the least worst option and walked back to the table with their tray.

Mason spotted him out of the corner of his eye. "Dad, watch my dismount! Here goes…"

"I see you, Mace. Be careful—I mean, watch out for the *bad* guys!"

Mason brought his knees to his chest, kicked both feet in front of him, and landed in a squatting position in front of James.

"Hi-ya!"

James's eyes were glued to Mason while he used his peripheral vision to spread their feast across the table. "Whoa…nice double jump front kick!"

"Dad, that was awesome. Come and jump with me. Let's fight the bad guys together! We could be the dynamic duo. I'll be Batman and you can be Robin!"

The boys scarfed their food while Mason shared the highlights of his superhero training. Then he began his well-defensed plea for more time.

"OK, bud, ten more minutes," James said. "Then we go." James reached over the table and gave Mason a smack on the butt. "Now go get 'em."

*This kid is like the Energizer Bunny. I wish I had half his energy. Heck, I'm going to need it! Once I get him to bed, I'll need to pull together these latest findings, and then I should be good to go for tomorrow…I wonder if Suzy is with Pops yet.*

He tapped a text to Suzy.

We're headed home in a few. Give Dad a hug from me, OK? Luv U, sweets.

"Did you have fun, bud?" James asked.

"Yeah, Dad, it was awesome! You should have come in with me."

"Next time, bud. Next time..."

Mason swigged his gigantic lemonade as they walked toward the exit.

"This place is *awesome!* Thank you, Dad!"

"You're welcome, son. I wish we could do this all the time!"

"Really, Dad?"

"Really!"

"Well, then how about tomorrow after school?"

*This kid never ceases to amaze me. Well, I can't blame him for asking for what he wants. That skill will serve him well as an adult, but I just don't want him to expect that he will always get what he wants, when he wants it. Or is that just a limiting belief of mine? I wish I would ask for what I want more often...*

James watched as Mason strutted toward the door, punching and kicking invisible attackers from all sides.

*I know that he's only going to be this age once and we should have more of these experiences, but I just have so much going on. I wish work was a little slower so I could catch my breath. I can't believe what happened to Bill. It just proves that it can happen to anyone.*

# FOUR

# The Downward Spiral
## Playing Below the Line

The minutes melted into hours as Mason finished his homework and James incorporated the latest findings for his morning meeting.

*It's great to see Mason having fun, and taking care of him isn't too tough. I'm sure I would have been digging through Luis's reports the entire evening if we hadn't gone trampolining. I just don't want to screw anything up tomorrow.*

James rounded the corner from his office to Mason's room and spotted the little man through the crack in the door.

"All right, bud. Last call. Time to put on PJs and brush your teeth."

"Aww, Dad, I'm not even tired!"

"Yeah, sure, it's time. Let's go." James nudged the door fully open and whisked Mason toward his dresser and then the bathroom. Mason marched erratically through his nightly routine and dove into bed.

"Dad, do you think I'm ever going to see Papa again?"

"Absolutely. I'm sure he's recovering now that Mama is taking care of him."

"I don't want Papa to die. I'll miss him. I *love* Papa…and he promised we would finish our chess game from Christmas!"

James and Mason prayed for Papa, Nana, and Suzy too.

"Good night, bud. See you in the morning. Mwah!" James planted a big kiss on Mason's forehead.

"Good night, Dad."

Mason struggled to keep his eyes open until they fluttered and finally closed.

James smiled and quietly exited the room.

*James, you are Super Daddy! You scored a couple dozen points by taking Mason to the trampolines. You scored a couple hundred more by keeping your cool at the doctor's office, and you crushed it at work today. You're awesome, baby!*

James continued to congratulate himself as he headed toward the kitchen.

*OK, I'll make coffee for the morning, take out the trash, and fill the dishwasher, and then I can take a moment for myself…*

After a quick twenty-minute burst, James plunked down in his favorite leather La-Z-Boy and let out a giant yawn.

*Phew…Suzy makes taking care of Mason, organizing our home, and excelling in her job look easy! I mean, it's nice to experience a day in her life once in a while, but it sure does feel good to not think about anything for a second.*

As he pulled back on the faux-wood handle to put the footrest up, his phone flashed.

Is Mason in bed yet? Can you talk?

James tapped out his response.

Yep, just put him down. Taking a moment to collect my thoughts.

Suzy called immediately.

"There's my girl. Hi, sweetie," James said, relaxing into his seat.

"Hey, how was your night with Mason?"

"Awesome. We had a great time playing superheroes at the trampoline park. I was just thinking what a great job you do for our family! For Mason, me, your job, and Pops. How is Pops, anyway?"

"He is in good spirits, but he hasn't been taking care of himself. He hasn't been working out, and his cholesterol is way too high. Mom and I spent the last hour talking about how she can start to make better food choices for them. It's amazing how little they know about health and nutrition."

Her words triggered James's looming frustration.

"Oh, yeah," Suzy added, "how was your visit with the doctor?"

*My visit…what do I tell her? Just take it slow and don't get crazy.*

"Well, I thought my appointment was with Dr. Collins, but she is on maternity leave. I didn't even know she was pregnant."

"Yeah, she's been trying for the past few years. So what did you find out?"

*Watch yourself, James. Don't step in the bear trap!*

"Honestly, the replacement doctor was rude. She had no bedside manner. I don't know why Dr. Collins let someone like that into her practice!"

"Oh, I'm sorry, James. It can't be that bad. I know you have been cutting down on your nighttime snacking. What were the results of your blood test?"

*I know she's going to be upset. Stay calm. You know she's had a big day, so just keep it light. I'm sure she already knows, so here goes…*

"She said my good cholesterol is too low, and my bad cholesterol is too high."

"Well, what is it?"

"226…"

"226? How could it be so high? We eat an English muffin or oatmeal every morning, and I make a healthy dinner every night! My cholesterol is 170. What are you eating when we're not together that's raising your cholesterol fifty-six points?"

"I don't know. I make good choices…"

James knew what she was going to ask before she even asked it.

"James, what did you and Mason have for dinner?"

"Uh, Mason had a hot dog, and I had a chicken sandwich."

"Was it breaded or grilled?"

"I don't remember."

"You don't remember? Did you have anything else?"

"Well, yeah, Mason and I each had a fry and a large lemonade."

"Listen, James, I think you are missing the point. Your cholesterol is too high. You haven't been getting to the gym. You're eating on the run, and I know you're stressed because you keep snapping at us for no reason…and lately you've been super sarcastic too!"

"Suzy, I thought you would be on my side!"

"I am on your side, but lately you've been missing the point. I get it. Sometimes the timing hasn't been right, or the delivery was not to your liking, but you need to stop shooting the messenger and start listening to the message! You need to assume positive intent!"

James rolled his eyes. *"Assume positive intent?" Pssh. Dr. Doubtful has no bedside manner, and now Suzy starts lecturing me. What's going on today? Is everyone against me?*

"James, what do you weigh?"

"What does it matter?"

"James, don't get defensive. I'm just trying to help."

"Uh-huh."

"What's wrong? Lately you only hear what you want to, and then you tune out. Great husbands and leaders appreciate all types of feedback. They don't just pick and choose the feedback that affirms their beliefs. They assume positive intent."

*I don't need this! I've been crushing it all day, and I've got more to do before I can hit the sack. I can't believe she is piling on now too!*

"James, I know you are frustrated, but I want you to know that no matter how much you weigh, I still love you. I'm tough on you because I want to grow old with you. I don't want a health surprise with you too."

James squirmed in the La-Z-Boy until it released a plastic squeal.

"Seeing Dad helpless has been a game changer for me," Suzy went on. "I don't want to fight with you about this. When I get back, we'll figure out a plan to get you back to the gym and to make better food choices when you're away from home. I want to keep you around for a long time, James. I have good intentions too!"

"It's just been a long day. I need time to process what the doctor said, what you are saying, and what the rest of the world is screaming at me."

"I understand, James. Just remember, I'm on your side."

"I know you are, and I need you on my side. Good night."

"Good night, James."

James placed his face in his hands and massaged his forehead with his fingertips.

Assume positive intent? *Why can't people just make it easy for me? I know I was pretty salty with the doctor, but she definitely needs some emotional-intelligence training. I'm not happy being twenty pounds heavier. I have less energy and less patience, and I'm way more stressed. I thought I was hiding my stress, but I guess I'm not hiding it very well. I just wish I could get the old James back again!*

## FIVE

# Jumping the Gun
## When Intentions ≠ Results

James went head down for another two hours, checking e-mail and reviewing the latest call-center reports until he fell asleep with them littered across his chest.

The next morning was a blur. He dropped Mason off at school and tried to shake off his residual thoughts about the doctor, his conversation with Suzy, and his many excuses.

"Stay with me, James," he said aloud. "Come on…focus!"

He pulled into the first parking spot, and the underside of the car scraped the concrete curb. He winced as he eased the car into reverse.

*Ouch…I hope today starts to turn around, because if things keep going the way they have been, I'll be out of a job…or worse!*

James unbuckled his seat belt and strode across the freshly seal-coated parking lot. Emily, Mr. Raven's executive assistant, met him inside.

"Hi, James, glad you made it! Mr. Raven is excited to meet with you," she said with a smile. "Please, follow me."

*Excited to meet with me? All right! It's about time things started going my way.*

"I'm grateful to be here, Emily."

"Mr. Raven's office is right down this hallway, the last door on the right. Can I get you anything to drink before I take you there?"

James only half heard her offer of hospitality because he was distracted by the sea of beige cubicles. The buzz of the room reminded him of a beehive, with the worker bees busy within the confines of their own honeycomb.

"Um, no thanks. I'm all set."

James heart raced as they approached Mr. Raven's office.

"Mr. Raven, James has arrived, sir."

"Great! Welcome to our humble abode." They shook hands, and Mr. Raven motioned to a table in the corner of his strategically arranged office.

"Thank you," James remarked as he snapped back to reality.

"So, James, this is your meeting. How do you want to get started?"

"Well, I've reviewed the data, and I think I have some ideas on how we can improve your numbers."

"You've reviewed the data? What data, James?"

"Well, Mr. Raven, I'm a bit of an overachiever. I took the liberty of running the past two years' worth of production reports for your office. I also pulled comparative reports from the other customer call centers and did some digging into the initiatives those offices implemented to improve their numbers…"

"Hmm, you surprised me by being so prepared. I thought the purpose of this meeting was to get to know each other and for me to answer your questions regarding the particulars of this office, but it's your show. What else do you know?"

*Take it easy, James. Don't jump the gun! But he does seem interested, so I'll share a little more of my rationale to gauge his interest...*

"From what I've seen, your customer satisfaction numbers are fair. However"—James paused—"it looks like your call times are on the rise and your severity numbers are spiking."

"Hmm, the numbers do reflect that. Why do you suppose that is?"

"I don't know for sure, but it appears that over the past two years, your call times have increased while other centers' call times have steadily decreased. Anything you can share that would help my understanding?"

"Well, James, I've been at Restoration Insurance for the past thirteen years and have spent the past ten years in this office. I've seen a lot of revolutionary ideas come and go, but I've found that *nothing* can replace great employees."

Mr. Raven paused to calm himself and select the appropriate response.

James, struggling with the silence, jumped in again. "I agree, Mr. Raven; it all depends on the people. They are the brand to the customer and can be the linchpin to achieving our goals!"

"James, I think you are onto something. Enlighten me."

"In digging into the changes at other offices, I see that no major differences exist between your site and the other locations. Therefore, I'm assuming it's an issue with your managers, your frontline employees, or both."

"I hope you have some direct experience and data that bring you to that conclusion, James."

*He seems impressed. This is going better than I planned! I know I should be listening more, but he keeps asking questions, so he must want to know...*

"Based on my evaluation, I recommend addressing the bottom

ten percent of staff and beginning an overhaul of your manager training and new-employee on-boarding program. By being more results focused, you can drive down call time, increase call volume, and ultimately achieve better results."

James took a breath, the first one in ten minutes, and then looked at Mr. Raven, who happened to be smiling.

"I see. Your suggestion seems simple: cut the bottom ten percent of employees and overhaul training, hiring, and on-boarding, and I should expect a decrease in call times within three months. Correct?"

"Well, kind of, but I didn't say cut the bottom ten percent. And it could take two full quarters to actualize the results."

After what seemed like an eternity, Mr. Raven sat up straight and glared past James and out the window.

*Uh-oh. Something is not right…*

"James, I've seen many a young buck strut in here with their innovative ideas. They guarantee to transform our results in short order. While I'm glad you were promoted on the basis of your merits and your knowledge of headquarters, this is not headquarters."

*I think this is going off the rails…*

"Tell me, how much research did you do on this office before you developed your current opinions?" Mr. Raven repeatedly tapped the desk with his index finger.

James stammered, "Well, I did some benchmarking against other field offices with similar client demographics, discussed it with a few of my peers, crunched the data, and formulated some ideas."

"Sounds like none! Listen, James, in this office, we are a work family, and we've been through tremendous change over the past two years. I know many of our folks are still struggling to incorporate the last round of technology mandated by headquarters."

Mr. Raven scowled and pointed east toward the head office.

"That technology has spiked the stress levels of every soul here because it doesn't allow us to serve the customer in the way we had previously! My people are doing the best they can."

"Mr. Raven, I wasn't trying to insult your people or your leadership—"

The ring of the phone interrupted the growing tension of their conversation. Gazing at the caller ID, Mr. Raven saw it was the call he had been expecting.

"James, I need to take this call; it's urgent. Do you mind seeing yourself out?"

*Do I mind seeing myself out? Oh, man, I jumped the gun and really messed up. How am I going to recover from this?*

James nodded good-bye while Mr. Raven picked up the phone.

"Hello, Mr. Anderson? Yes, I can talk. I do have the updates from our last leadership meeting. Our tiger team dug into the data and discovered…"

Still stunned, James slithered out as Mr. Raven's conversation began to fade. He walked past the sea of honeycombs and out to his car. Resting his head on the steering wheel, he began replaying the conversation.

*That was brutal! I don't know exactly where it went off the rails, but I'll give him some time to digest our conversation, and I'll schedule a call with him in the morning. Maybe he's just in denial? Well, I'd better grab something to eat on my way back to the office, because Val will be looking for a project update, and then I have my one-on-one with Bob. Today can't possibly get any worse.*

## SIX

# Tightening the Leash
Who'da Thunk It?

J ames arrived at headquarters and, upon reaching the elevator, saw a sign:

"Closed for Maintenance"

*Brilliant! Who is the genius who scheduled maintenance during the workday? Looks like I'll have to take the stairs.*

James popped the handle on the heavy steel door and proceeded up the stairs. Short of breath, he reached the third floor.

*Maybe I am a little out of shape. I don't remember it taking so much effort. I guess it's been a while since I took the stairs.*

James logged into the system and simultaneously retrieved his voice mails. For the next several hours, he went head down, catching up on e-mail and reviewing his thoughts from the morning meeting, until a call from his boss interrupted him.

"Hi, Bob. What's up?"

"James, I need you to come down to my office immediately!"

*Immediately? Oh boy, I wonder if he heard what happened this morning. No, he couldn't have heard it that quick. Maybe he just needs to reschedule our one-on-one.*

When James got to his boss's office, Bob said, "James, have a seat. I just had lunch with an old friend, Chris Raven, and he shared with me your conversation from this morning. Tell me, James, from your perspective, what was the purpose of that meeting?"

*Oh, shoot, his old friend Chris Raven? They knew each other? I wonder what he told Bob. I hope he had a little time to digest our conversation before he threw me under the bus. Well, here goes.*

"Uh, well, I, uh, wanted to meet with Mr. Raven to ask him a few questions about his office and learn how they do things…"

James paused, scanning Bob's face intently for his reaction, but Bob, an avid poker player, was stone faced.

"And how do you think the meeting went, James?"

"Uh, it could have gone better. I might have jumped the gun a bit."

"What do you mean, you might have jumped the gun?"

"Well, I wanted to show Mr. Raven I had done a significant amount of homework and preparation leading into our meeting. I knew that his results were subpar compared to the other call centers' and that something needed to be done. I was trying to impress him with my knowledge, but he might have felt that I insulted his leadership a little bit."

Bob inhaled deeply and deliberately chose his words.

"James, I promoted you into this position to help consult and provide support to our internal clients. While I appreciate your passion, nothing beats curiosity. You can't go into a meeting with an experienced leader and assume you know what they need to do based on some printed reports. Heck, you don't even know what they have done or are doing. That's irresponsible. You know better than that! If you would have started by being curious, you would have discovered that they are having some seriously complex challenges."

"Bob, I made a mistake. I just wanted to help them fix their issues. I had good intentions…"

"I know you have good intentions, and I'll take the blame for this one. I've given you too much freedom, and I let you get ahead of yourself. I'm going to need to tighten your leash to make sure this doesn't happen again."

*Tighten my leash? What does he mean? This can't be good.*

"Listen, James, you're going to start by getting your head out of those comparative reports. You're going to march back over to the call center and start talking to some real people to better understand their current situation. God gave you two ears and one mouth. Use them proportionately! Do I make myself clear?"

*Oh, man, Bob is pissed. I can't believe I fell into Mr. Raven's trap. I had good intentions and just said too much too quickly. Sometimes I'm such an idiot!*

"Totally clear, Bob. I'm sorry to disappoint you."

"Don't worry about disappointing me! You should be more worried about the loss of reputation with our client. Your first impression put you in a hole that you might not be able to climb out of. I suggest you get abundantly clear on your intentions for this next visit."

Bob slammed his notebook closed and pointed toward the door.

"That's it, James. We're done for today. No more talking. It's time to *show* me that you understand and to change your behavior accordingly. Got it?"

"Yes, sir! Abundantly clear." James rose from his chair, turned, and walked toward the door. As he squeezed the brushed-silver handle, Bob continued.

"Nine o'clock tomorrow morning! You are scheduled for a series of meetings to better understand what is really going on at their facility from multiple perspectives. You have one chance to make this right. Don't mess it up!"

*Figures. I make one mistake, and the guy happens to be a close personal friend of my boss. Who'da thunk it?*

James slunk back to his desk and halfheartedly poked around his inbox. The remainder of the afternoon crept slowly as he replayed his disappointing morning.

*OK, James. Good try this morning, but what would you do different next time? Well, I'd start by creating a relationship with Mr. Raven. I could have asked what they are trying to accomplish and probed a little more to discover his biggest challenges. I could have shared my intention for the meeting and been more transparent with him. I wish I could get a do-over!*

# SEVEN

# Bring On the Villains
## Meet Craven and the Storm

James glanced at the clock in the upper corner of his screen. *Whoa…it's time to pick up Mason already? That's OK. My brain is spinning, and I have a million things to do, but I'm not making much progress anyway. Mr. Raven and Bob are totally in my head. I need to get them out!*

James was lost in his thoughts as he drove to pick up Mason.

*It's so frustrating! I try so hard, and yet it feels like my best just isn't good enough. Why do I do this to myself? Why do I try so hard and then put myself in a hole? Am I sick in the head? Do I like this kind of punishment? Come on, James, it's time to shift gears. It's time to transition to being Super Daddy again. Mason is going to demand all of your attention. You need to be ready.*

James parked the SUV and walked briskly into the school.

"Hey, bud! I missed you!"

They pounded fists with an exaggerated explosion of fireworks.

"Hi, Dad! I missed you too! What are we going to do today?"

"I don't know, Mason. I'm thinking we can head home, heat up some dinner, and chill at home for the night."

"That's boring! Can you take my bag, Dad?"

"Yeah, it does sound a little boring, but Daddy had a big day at work, and he needs to take it a little easy tonight, OK?"

The two strapped into the SUV and eased back into traffic.

"When does Mom get back?"

"Not soon enough, bud. Why are you asking?"

"Well, Mom always plans to do something on Tuesday after school. Sometimes we go to the library or to watch the monkeys at the zoo."

"Honestly, I need to go home. I've been beaten up too much today."

"You got beat up at work today? What happened?"

"Well, I didn't get physically beaten up, but I did take a verbal pounding."

"Did you fight back?"

"Well, kind of. After I dropped you off this morning, I met with a client, and things got off to a rocky start..."

*What am I doing? Am I trying to share my crazy day with Mason? He doesn't care. Well, maybe if I put it in a way he can understand...*

"That's when this villain jumped out of his hero costume."

"Didn't you know he was a villain in disguise when you met him?"

"Maybe I had a hunch. At first he was relaxed, supportive, and friendly, but he quickly revealed a stubborn and hesitant side. He baited me into telling my super secrets, and then he struck out of nowhere. I was stunned and couldn't get my bearings. I tried to recover, but he pinned me down and didn't give me a chance to breathe!"

"He sounds scary, Daddy! Are you OK?"

"Yeah, I'm OK. I just wanted to create a great first impression, but he kept asking questions and baited me into answering them."

"He tricked you into sharing your super secrets, and then he showed you a different side?"

"Exactly! It was like he wanted to hear what I thought would help his team, but when I highlighted the hero's path he got defensive."

"Did he try to cover his anger with a smile?"

"Kind of. I think you are on to something. Chris Raven is hesitant, plodding, and stubborn. He appears to care about people and relationships, but then, without provocation, he pounces, paralyzing his victims, rendering them helpless."

"Dad, I think you might have met the cautious and steady villain they call Craven. Yep, that's him, Dad. He's the evil villain Craven!"

"Craven, you say? That would make sense.

"Then, after I escaped, I was ambushed by someone who I thought was a friend. He lured me into his office, and with my defenses down, he exposed my vulnerability and pounded me with his feedback. The surprise attack still has me reeling!"

"Tell me more about this villain, Dad."

"Well, this person is confident, to the point, and sometimes short tempered. He is assertive, task focused, and results oriented. He loves being in control and is always looking for a challenge. He is competitive but can quickly become blunt and authoritative!"

"Oh no! He lured you in and attacked when you were vulnerable?"

"Yeah, he hates complications, waiting, and delays. He is quick to judge and strikes without feelings. You think everything is fine, and then all of a sudden, he lashes out and leaves you helpless and flailing to recover."

"When he pauses, you think everything is fine, but it's just the calm before the storm. That's it, Dad! Let's call him the Storm!"

"The Storm, huh? I can see that. He is driving, unyielding, and overbearing. He tries to manipulate you with his quick thinking and sweeping assumptions. Then when you least expect it, he pounds you with his punishing storm."

"Yep, Dad, that's the Storm! I can't believe you had to fight two villains today and you're alive to tell the story. You are awesome!"

*Well, maybe I am embellishing the Bob story a bit, but it's kind of true.*

"I'm glad we aren't villains, Mason. We are superheroes!"

"Let's get those villains and make them pay for their evil deeds!"

James peered into the rearview mirror and watched Mason rage into a fury, his face tense and his fists darting in all directions.

*Have I gone too far? I was just trying to have a little fun with the boy. I was only playing. How can I make this better?*

"Mason?" James waved into the rearview mirror as he tried to get his son's attention. "Hey, bud. I deal with these types of bad guys all the time. Thank you, but I know how to handle them."

"Oh, Dad, guys like that get me so angry!"

"Don't worry. Daddy has a plan for making it all better."

The boys arrived home, played video games, heated up a frozen vegetable pizza, and went through their nighttime routine. Then James let out a sigh as he closed Mason's door.

*I'm glad he is finally in bed. That little dude really has some spunk, and he sure loves his daddy! I guess I need to choose what I say to my mini-me. He picks up on my energy and gets all riled up—just like Suzy! Oh yeah, Suzy. I need to check in and see how she is doing. Honestly, I don't know how she does it. She wears her work hat, then she puts on her mommy hat, then her wife hat, and now her daughter hat. No wonder she was so upset about me ruining our first couple days of vacation.*

James glanced down at his watch: nine o'clock.

*Well, it's still pretty early. Once I check in with Suzy, I can have some time to process the day and plan for tomorrow. I need to make sure I don't dump on Suzy. Promise me you won't go there, James, OK?*

James tapped out a text message to Suzy.

Big day! Thinking of you. Want to talk in 15 mins?
Love & Kisses!

James slid his phone back into his pocket and headed downstairs to prepare Mason's lunch for the next day, clean up from dinner, and rest his eyes for a few minutes.

Greeted by the familiar buzz against his leg, James answered Suzy's call.

"Hi, love," James said. "I've been thinking about you."

"Oh yeah? How so?"

"Just how much of an amazing wife, mom, and daughter you are."

"James, that's so nice. You must really be struggling over there."

They laughed together.

"Yeah, today has been a little rough, but I can handle it. I'm Super Daddy!"

"Oh, James, I'm sure I don't want to know what you two are up to."

"Honestly, Suzy, it's all good over here. Nothing we can't handle. How are you doing over there? Is Dad improving? How is Mom handling all this?"

"I'm fine. Dad's improving each day. I'm trying to help Mom understand what she can do to help with Dad's recovery, but she's kind of clueless. I'm anxious about getting back to our life. How did your big meeting go today?"

*You've been doing good so far, James. Don't take the bait...*

"Well, the meeting didn't go how I'd planned, and I found out that the client and Bob have some shared history that I wasn't aware of."

"Shared history? What do you mean?"

"When I got back into the office, Bob wanted to meet with me. That's when I found out they were good friends. I guess they had lunch scheduled for today, and our meeting became the main topic of their conversation."

"Oh, James, I'm sorry. I know you spent a lot of time preparing. Could it just be a misunderstanding?"

*A misunderstanding? Seriously? I was the one thrown under the bus. Well, if she really wants to know what happened...*

"Suz, we got off on the right foot, but then it just went south from there. He started asking questions and baited me into telling him what I thought was wrong with his office. He kept asking questions, and I kept answering. Then he got an urgent call and dismissed me."

"That doesn't make any sense. Could you be missing something?"

"I wish I was, but that's how it went down. Bob caught wind of it at lunch and gave me the ultimatum to head back over there tomorrow morning for a series of meetings starting at nine."

"What might be going on that you don't know about, James?"

*What doesn't she get? It's not me, it's them. They're the crazy ones!*

"What might be going on is an alternate universe where villains attack heroes for no reason. Mason and I talked about it on the way home. Our little dude got a little too hyped when I told him about how they attacked me. He even named them Craven and the

Storm."

"*James!* You did not dump your issues on our son and drag him into your insane world of heroes and villains! He is just a boy. He doesn't know what really happened. He believes your exaggerated stories and thinks you're telling the truth. He takes on your frustration, and it's just not fair!"

"Exaggerated stories? I am telling the truth! What's not fair is what I had to endure today with those villains. They attacked me for no reason, and now I have to fall on my sword to satiate their endless egos."

"James, don't you remember the conversation we had last night?"

"Yeah…which one?"

"The one about assuming positive intent. I think you're getting caught up in your emotions, being sarcastic, and exaggerating whatever happened today."

"I am not!"

"I *know* you are! You do it all the time with me. You tell me some James-sized version of reality. You get me hooked and wanting to help, and I end up just taking on your frustration, anger, and bitterness. Then you leave me feeling all crappy while you move on to anyone else who will listen, including our seven-year-old son!"

"Suzy, come on…"

"Come on nothing, James. This has been coming for a long time. You need to hear this. Stop shooting the messenger and start looking at the situation from the perspective of others. You need to start assuming positive intent, or the tough life you think you have is going to get much more difficult!"

*Is she threatening me? She had better watch herself, or…take a chill, James. You knew this was a no-win situation. She's just hot and needs time to cool off.*

"I shouldn't have mentioned it. I should've kept my big mouth shut."

"Should've, would've, could've. I suggest you quit being so selfish."

The line went dead.

*What is going on today? Have I woken up in some bizarro world? I just need to escape this insanity. I'll lie down on the couch and decompress with a little inspiration. Unbelievable—is this classic Batman episode #43? The one where Batman battles the Penguin? Perfect!*

James's eyelids fluttered and then closed for good. His mind replayed the lowlights from his horrific day as he drifted off to sleep.

*The Storm*                    *Craven*

## EIGHT

# The Drift

## Hero Habit: Assume Positive Intent

"James, be a good boy and stay here while Mommy does a little snorkeling."

"OK, Mommy."

"I'm just going to tie your raft to this rock, and you'll be able to see the fish under the water too. I'll be right here; just call me if you need something. OK, James?"

"All right."

The sun beat down on the blue Caribbean water and on James's small inflatable raft.

*Wow, I can see all the way to the bottom. I wonder how many fish are down there. And look at all of those crabs scooting across the rocks. I hope they don't untie my rope. I bet I could catch one of those crabs, or maybe I could catch a whole bunch. I'm going to try when I get back on shore. Boy, it sure is hot!*

"Hey, Mom. Mom!"

"Yes, James?"

"What do you see down there?"

"It's *amazing!* I see hundreds of fish with the brightest colors you've ever seen. There are some yellow and red ones and some blue and green ones too."

"Can I use your mask?"

"Not right now, James. Be a good boy and stay in the raft. When Daddy comes down, you can play on the shore. I know you want to try to catch some of those crabs."

"I'll be a good boy, but I wanna see the fish too!"

James watched his mom make several passes through the shallows with only her snorkel above the water. She was mesmerized by the beauty below the surface.

*When I get back to shore, I'm going to catch a whole bucket of crabs, and we can eat them for dinner. I'll call the mission "Operation Bucket of Crabs." Boy, they sure are quick, so I'll need to have a stick too, and maybe a shovel so I don't get pinched by their claws. Oh, look at that huge one hiding inside the rock...*

James's gaze shifted to the sky as he followed a dozen seagulls until they became specks and disappeared into the distance. Then he turned toward shore and shouted.

"Mom? Mom! *MOM!*"

*Oh no. I'm getting farther away from shore! Maybe I can pull the rope and drag myself back. I'll just give the rope a tug and...uh-oh.*

The rope fell gently from the rock and dropped into the water. His raft, having just cleared the jutting rock face, began to pick up speed in the current.

"Mooooooommmmmmmmmmmmmm..."

James's words fell dead upon the rolling waves.

*What am I going to do?*

James looked into the water and saw a large fish underneath his raft.

*Was that a fin? It's a shark! I bet he's circling me and wants to* eat me for dinner. I can't jump out, or he will eat me before I get to shore!

*"MOOOOOOOOOMMMMMMMMMMM…"*

James could no longer see the detail of the crabs on the shore. His mother's snorkel was somewhere off in the distance, and the current was hastening his departure out to sea. James looked out the other side of the raft and saw the vast ocean and the silhouette of a small island.

*I wonder if Mom will ever hear me. I'll wait until she comes up again, and then I'll scream really loud. How could she forget about me? She loves me…I think. I'm so scared. Please come up, Mommy. Please!*

She surfaced off in the distance, cleared her mask and snorkel, and quickly submerged again. She was oblivious to his screams.

*MMMMMMMMMMMMMMMMAAAAAAAAAA…"*

*Why isn't she listening? If she doesn't look soon, I'm going to drift over to that island. I'll grow up alone, eating coconuts, and I'll never get to see my family again…*

"Oh, God, please help me. Please have my mommy raise her head and look for me. I promise that I'll never be bad again! I'll do anything…Please!"

***

James awoke suddenly, covered in sweat, seeing only the flickering light from the TV.

"Where am I? What's going on?"

He gasped, swallowed, and wiped the beading sweat from his brow.

*It was only a dream, but it felt so real. Actually, I remember that place. It really happened. I remember. I drifted too far and almost lost my family. I'm almost losing my family again. I've got to do something. I've got to stop drifting away from them and from who I am at my core!*

James sat up with a mixture of tears and sweat streaming down his cheeks.

*I have so much to be grateful for, and yet I keep finding the bad in everything. I judge people who disagree with my ideas and perspective. I discount their feedback unless it supports my actions. I've been a villain, and I'm tired of it. I want to be a hero!*

James's expression suddenly changed from sadness to elation.

*Heroes live by habits that enable them to overcome any challenge without losing integrity with their values. Knowingly or unknowingly, Suzy taught me a hero habit: assume positive intent...*

James sprang to his feet and fumbled for the light switch. He searched for anything he could use to capture his revelation. He spotted a notepad sticking out of a partially zipped compartment of Mason's backpack. He flipped open the cover and began to write.

# HERO HABIT
# ASSUME POSITIVE INTENT

## GOOD INTENTIONS ≠ GOOD RESULTS

I need to stop thinking that the world is out to get me. I'm giving away my power to my inner villain and he's causing me to push people away and ASSUME NEGATIVE INTENT!

I want to believe that people have good intentions, but I'm struggling to see the GOOD in what Bob, Mr. Raven and the Doctor are trying to tell me. I'm caught up in the SWIRL!

I know that people's behaviors aren't always indicative of their intentions. I'm just so overwhelmed and I'm struggling to appreciate their feedback. I need to find a way to discover their hidden intent before jumping to conclusions.

Hero Tip:
Heroes step into FEAR to overcome FAILURE. They choose UNDERSTANDING over BLAME in an attempt to ensure every team member contributes their BEST!

Heroes are good finders who always find a way to ASSUME POSITIVE INTENT

# NINE

# Bloom Where You're Planted
## Hero Habit: Design a Winnable Game

James took a few minutes to study the employees as they entered the call center. Most, but not all, seemed to be smiling. Then he entered the lobby and took a few moments to soak in the culture.

*I hope today's better than yesterday.*

The door to the office swung open with great enthusiasm.

"Hi, James. I'm Stephanie. How is your day going so far?"

"All right, I guess," James mumbled as he followed Stephanie back through the matrix of cubes to her own honeycomb.

"Well, that's not going to make it around here," Stephanie responded, furrowing her brow and pointing to the empty chair to her left.

"Excuse me?" James was now paying attention.

"You heard me," she replied, tugging the handle of a gray metallic drawer next to James's leg. She pulled out a second headset and began unraveling the cords.

"I hope you're better than all right when you leave today."

Stephanie grinned playfully and turned to face the dual

computer screens that dominated her desk.

"James, here is your headset; you're in listen mode, OK? And just so we're on the same page, please do not speak unless we are on mute. Your presence should go unnoticed by our customers."

"Yes, ma'am."

"I quickly review the clients' situation before I call them back. I look through these four windows and visualize their situation."

Her cursor glided through the customer information, date of initial contact, comments from the previous call, value offered for the car, and next steps.

She paused and sat up straight in her chair. "Uh-oh…we were supposed to call this person back, but it appears the follow-up task wasn't triggered." She looked at James. "I don't imagine they're happy. This might be a tough one."

Taking a deep breath, she fixed her eyes on the screen and whispered to herself, "What does winning look like?"

She glanced at James. "Are you ready for a little baptism by fire?"

"Sure. Let's go."

Stephanie initiated the call. "Hi, Mr. Almeida. This is Stephanie from Restoration Insurance, where we protect you from life's uncertainties. I'm here to resolve your claim."

"It's about time! I've been waiting for your call for over a week. Honestly, I don't have much hope left. The last person sure couldn't help me…"

*Tough room. I wonder what she's going to do with that.*

"Mr. Almeida, I apologize for our lack of response. You're right; we should have gotten back to you much sooner. I'll do my best to make it up to you."

"The delay has created a lot of inconvenience for my wife and I."

"I'm sorry, Mr. Almeida. I'd like to resolve this for you today. Do you mind if I ask you a few additional questions to verify the details of the accident?"

James raised his eyebrows, his eyes open wide. *How is she taking on this situation with such grace? What's her secret?* James, formerly hunched, sat up in his chair.

For fifteen minutes, Stephanie reviewed every scratch and dent on the vehicle while allowing Mr. Almeida to be heard, not as a customer, but as a person. She asked him very specifically what he was looking to accomplish today and how she could make this situation right in his eyes.

*She's amazing! She's taking time to understand his needs while determining what matters most to him, and she's accomplishing her objectives as an employee of Restoration Insurance. She must have superpowers...*

"Thank you very much for your patience, Mr. Almeida. I'm sorry that our initial value offered for your damage was not to your liking and that we took so long to respond." Stephanie paused.

"Based on the additional details you provided today, I'm able to extend your rental coverage and add an additional fifty dollars to replace the gas you put in the car just before it was declared a total loss."

"But I need to get a replacement car ASAP, and we don't have that kind of money just lying around! We barely make ends meet..."

"Absolutely, Mr. Almeida. I can have one of my processors overnight you a check. You can start looking for a replacement car tonight, and we'll have a check delivered by ten tomorrow morning. Will that work for you?"

"You can do that?"

"Of course! I just wish we could have handled this a week ago."

"Honestly, my wife really loved that car. No matter what you offered, it wouldn't be anywhere near the sentimental value. I really appreciate you allowing me to let off some steam. Sorry I was so rude."

"No problem. I apologize for our lack of response and for the challenges it caused you and your spouse."

"Thank you, Stephanie. I'm glad I got to speak to you. I think I might need to consider switching the rest of my insurance needs to Restoration."

Stephanie's eyes lit up like a kid's in a candy store.

"I'll have one of our local agents give you a call to discuss your request further. Is there anything else I can do for you today, Mr. Almeida?"

"Yes, one last thing. I'd like to get transferred to your supervisor, so I can tell her personally what a great job you've done!"

"Thank you for the offer, Mr. Almeida, but would you mind staying on the line to complete the feedback survey? I think that will give us both the result you are looking to create. I hope you find your next car tonight!" She hung up and glanced at James with a rosy smile that extended well beyond her face.

James sat quiet for a few moments, letting Stephanie bask in her victory, unsure whether he should speak or give her a high five.

"Stephanie, that was awesome! You took a situation that was bad from the start and made it a great experience for him. What's your secret?"

"James, there is no secret. I needed to understand what winning looked like for him so I could *design a winnable game.*"

*What is she talking about? This is work, not a game.*

"Winnable game?" James furrowed his brow and tilted his head at a subtle angle, much like the monkeys they visited at the zoo.

"Yes, sir. I needed to understand Mr. Almeida's biggest concern. Was it money? Did he want to make his wife happy? Or did he want to feel like he won the conversation? I had to uncover his needs so I could speak his language."

James, eyes fixed on Stephanie, hung on her every word.

"It's pretty simple. I took responsibility for our lack of communication, listened to his concerns, and offered an opportunity to solve his problem. He relaxed because I was no longer his opposition. I was his conduit to success. I knew what winning looked like, for him and for Restoration."

James turned his chair and looked her squarely in the eyes.

"So it sounds like you listened to what he wanted, asked questions to clarify his greatest need, and co-created a solution that you both could accept."

"Exactly!" She gave James a double thumbs-up. "I view situations through the lens of a game because I love to play games and I love to *win* games."

"Who doesn't?" asked James.

"But," Stephanie said, holding up her right index finger, "all games have rules and boundaries, which are not always obvious. So I spent extra time—time I didn't want to spend but needed to *invest*—in order to *win* the game.

"When he told me his biggest concern was to get a working vehicle, I had all the cards! I knew what had happened from his customer file. I knew his desired outcome. With the cards in hand, I knew we could resolve his issue. In that moment, he saw his light at the end of the tunnel, and I saw my win."

"Stephanie, why do you care so much?"

"Well, my parents taught me to bloom where I'm planted. They taught me that I can bloom even when things are crumbling around me. They taught me to have perseverance and inner joy no matter what I'm doing. They taught me that no task is too menial."

Stephanie paused and looked at the ground.

"In prior jobs I have done anything from handling a Madagascar cockroach to helping an elderly person go to the bathroom. I choose to find joy in every task I have ever done. My parents taught me that happiness is a choice.

"When I can help someone move forward in life and be happy, then I'm happy. At the end of the call, Mr. Almeida and I were both happy. We both won our respective games.

"I also know that for every unhappy customer, I have an opportunity to correct the situation. If I don't, it might bubble up to my managers, and they don't need one more thing on their desk," Stephanie said with a wink. "Or an unhappy customer could turn to social media, taking the situation viral—or worse, they could file a report with the Department of Insurance. All of those scenarios reflect poorly on us."

*She is onto something here. I'm onto something. I'm looking for heroes, and she shows up. Is it really that easy? I just assume positive intent, and my world becomes a legion of superheroes? Suzy's a...*

"Genius," James whispered under his breath.

"I don't know about 'genius,' James. It's just something that works, and I don't think much about it anymore. It's a habit!"

*Her agent referral definitely doesn't show up in the call-time metrics. Stephanie has some powerful beliefs that allow her to reframe any situation.*

Stephanie and James took several more calls together, and Stephanie continued to not only win but beat her high score on each call.

"That hour flew by, Stephanie. Thank you. You're a superhero!

I'm thankful I was able to experience you in action! Question: I've got a series of meetings remaining today, but would you mind if I gave you a call to help make sense of anything else that comes up?"

"Absolutely, James! You have my number. I would be honored."

James said good-bye and sped off to meet with several of Mr. Raven's direct reports and eventually with Mr. Raven himself.

*I can't believe this assume positive intent stuff is so easy. I wish they would have taught this in college, high school, or heck, maybe even in elementary school. I think I've discovered another hero habit: design a winnable game.*

James reached into his bag and began to write out his new hero habit...

# HERO HABIT
# DESIGN A WINNABLE GAME

Honestly, I haven't thought about what WINNING looks like lately. I know I need to be challenged, but I'm feeling more STRESSED than S-T-R-E-T-C-H-E-D!

I've been taking on too much and haven't relied on others for help. It seems like no matter how much time and effort I invest, I NEVER get to experience winning, and it's allowing my VILLAIN to THRIVE!

I need to start thinking of LIFE as a game! I need to figure out WHAT winning looks like, and then I can leverage my STRENGTHS. But why? What's my WHY? My WHY is my FUEL! When I understand my WHY, I understand my purpose, and I'll have something bigger than my alarm to wake up to in the morning. Once I know my WHAT & WHY, then I just need to figure out HOW, so I can take a strategic approach to WINNING!

Hero Tip:
Heroes design lives that maximize their STRENGTHS. They EMBRACE challenges instead of DREADING them. Heroes enjoy the daily struggles because they know it's their opportunity to BE THE HERO.

Heroes DESIGN their lives as A WINNABLE GAME!

## TEN

# Eating Crow
## Can I Get a Mulligan?

'm glad to see you again, James." Mr. Raven smiled, silently giving James kudos for returning to the scene of yesterday's crime.

"Thank you. I need to apologize for yesterday. I—"

"No need to apologize. Bob thinks very highly of you, and that's the reason I'm giving you a mulligan. Have a seat and tell me about your visit."

*Bob thinks highly of me? I'm shocked, based on the scolding he gave me yesterday. All right, James, let's stay on Chris's good side.*

"Well, my sit-along with Stephanie was enlightening, and thank you for setting up the meetings with your managers. They're quite diverse in their leadership style and experience."

"Absolutely. With the variety of work we do, we need a diversity of thought and perspective. Managing the breadth of diversity is a constant challenge."

"I can see that. But when you have people like Stephanie, it makes balancing the challenge that much easier, right?"

"What do you mean?"

"Well, I watched Stephanie work with a very difficult customer.

She was able to turn the situation completely around, not just once but several times. It was magic the way she discovered the customer's needs and created a winnable game for him and for us."

James quickened his pace as he tried to contain his enthusiasm about Stephanie's superpowers and his new hero habit.

"James, it sounds like you really enjoyed meeting with Stephanie."

"Absolutely, sir! If we could figure out how to clone her, then all of your problems would be solved."

James chuckled, but Mr. Raven's smile quickly faded.

*Oops. What did I say? It must have been about cloning Stephanie…*

"Listen, James, while Stephanie is a great person, you need to remain unbiased. You cannot be swayed by one-off stories or experiences. Using those to create recommendations or change existing processes is a trap. You must think of Stephanie as a data point in your research. An equally weighted data point. Then you need to focus on collecting more data from a variety of sources before jumping to a conclusion."

Mr. Raven shook his head disappointedly and then locked eyes with James.

"You're a young guy with a whole career ahead of you. I know you want to make an impact right away, but you can't discount the value of experience."

*I'm not that young, and I already have a significant amount of experience!*

"I guarantee you'll learn something from each of my people. If you take their knowledge, add insights from the other call centers, sprinkle in some of your innovative ideas, and refine them as you discover unexpected challenges, you'll have a solution that will impress even the toughest critics."

*Toughest critics—he must mean himself. Maybe he means Bob too. They were pretty tough on me yesterday, but Mr. Raven seems to be coming around today. I wonder if something else was going on to set him off yesterday.*

"I think I understand."

"Great! That's why I want you to come back tomorrow to meet with a few more of my leaders from the other side of the business and do another desk-side interview. Ashley is fairly new, and although I have yet to meet with her, I'm told her results are already near the top."

*OK, it looks like I'm coming back tomorrow. I'll have to reschedule the update meeting with Val, but that shouldn't be an issue. After tomorrow, I'll have all the data I need to put together a killer recommendation.*

"All right, James, I have a call with my VP, and I need a few minutes to prepare. I'll see you tomorrow, OK?"

James sprang from his seat and shook Mr. Raven's hand.

"Good luck with the call, and I'll be here at nine tomorrow!"

"James, if you don't have anything pressing back at the office, maybe you can stick around and observe how things operate around here."

# ELEVEN

# The Hero's Journey
## Hero Habit: Pay It Forward

O*h, man, this is great! I assume positive intent, and I'm instantly surrounded by heroes. Mr. Raven is coming around, and things are looking up for me. I'll take his advice and be a fly on the wall until I need to leave to pick up Mason.*

James scanned the field of cubicles, finding only one empty cube.

*Everyone sure looks busy.*

He examined the remnants of the previous cube owner.

*What do we have here? A floor diagram. It's always good to know where the bathroom is. Restoration's mission statement, a phone-extension listing, and their North Star: "People First—that includes you." I wonder what that means.*

James pulled out his laptop and began typing a message to Bob.

Subject: Thanks for the Mulligan

Bob,
Thanks for giving me a second chance. I started
the day with a desk-side interview that gave me a
different perspective. Then I had a few meetings with
Chris's managers and finished by meeting with Chris.

I'm going to stick around and see if I can catch a
glimpse of what really goes on behind the scenes. I'll
be back in the office tomorrow.

Cheers,
James

*Bob really saved my butt. I wonder what the history
is with him and Chris anyway. I'll ask him in our meeting tomorrow.
Oops, I almost forgot; I need to reschedule my update meeting with Val.
I'll just—whoa...*

James's thought was interrupted by a flurry of incoming e-mails.
*What happened? I'm buried! Imagine a world without e-mail. I
could talk with people and not have to guess what they're thinking.*

A muted chorus caused James to rise up from his chair like
a prairie dog and intently scan for its source. He homed in on
humming coming from the break room. As he walked closer, he
heard a chorus of "Happy Birthday" and noticed a small cake
surrounded by a group of folks.

An older woman stood at the table, staring beyond the cake.

"I'm glad I have you guys. Honestly, I went through a rough patch after my Eric passed away. We were married for twenty-one years. He's the only family I have. I mean had."

"Elizabeth, I know we will never replace Eric, but I want you to know that we are ecstatic to have you as part of our family. Our work family…"

*That voice sounds familiar. Who is that?*

As James rounded the corner, the man came into full view.

*Mr. Raven? How does he find the time to attend these easily skippable employee events? There must be something more to this guy than I thought.*

James returned to his temporary desk and worked feverishly for another ninety minutes. Then he began packing his bag.

*Mr. Raven appeared tough on the outside, but maybe he was just defending his people. I thought he was the villain, but maybe he saw me as the villain. He did say, "Whatever is most important to my people, I make it a priority." Maybe he was just being the defender of this kingdom, and he saw me as a threat.*

Walking down the hallway, James saw Emily exiting Mr. Raven's office with her purse hung over her shoulder.

"Good night, sir."

"Good night, Emily."

James slowed near Chris's office and noticed him looking toward the upper shelf of his bookcase.

"Excuse me, Mr. Raven. I just want to thank you for setting up my meetings today. They really helped expand my knowledge."

"No problem, James." Mr. Raven turned in his chair to face him. "Did you notice anything interesting while you were here?"

"After you *volun*-told me to stick around?"

Mr. Raven's laugh was contagious, and both he and James

smiled.

"I thought you would understand my 'implied' request." Chris motioned with air quotes.

"Well, I noticed your North Star pinned to the cube wall."

"Absolutely. The North Star is our daily reminder about *what* and *who* we are committed to; *why* we do it, which is our purpose; and, just as important, *how* we go about achieving our daily activities."

"But we are a metrics-based culture. What do you mean exactly?"

"Excellent question, James! We are very focused on our goals and metrics, but just focusing on metrics is not how we achieve results. Our North Star allows us to behave differently in achieving those results. For example, putting people first is something that I have always focused on, and I want each of us to keep that in the forefront of our decisions. But early in my career, I used to be a big softy."

"A big softy? What do you mean?"

"I used to avoid confrontation at all cost and try to make other people happy. It came at the expense of my own happiness and our business results. I've learned that there is a balance in putting people first. We need good people to deliver great customer service, and those good people have a myriad of challenges beyond these walls. I realized that most people want to do good, but a few individuals just don't. They don't want help and won't change until something extreme happens. I used to try to help them more than they wanted to help themselves."

"I saw you in the break room celebrating Elizabeth's birthday. I was wondering how you make time for those types of events."

"There's a balance, James. It used to consume a huge chunk

of my time, but now I've built reserves with my people, and they know I have good intentions. They know that first and foremost we have a business to run. In the past, I didn't understand that, and I learned that lesson the hard way. Sometimes we have to make tough decisions to outsource or let people go, but in the end, we make all our business decisions through our people-first filter. My people know that I have their back, and they reciprocate by working hard and staying challenged."

"I guess I might have triggered you when I came in here stereotyping your people as underperforming."

"You sure did. I think our people are great, and I'll do my best to make sure they have the tools, skills, and resources they need to be successful. Listen, James, *how you do anything is how you do everything.* If you come in here making assumptions and hasty decisions, people will lose respect, and if they don't believe you have their best interests in mind, they will mentally quit long before they physically quit. The worst type of employee is the energy drainer who complains about everything that is going wrong but who won't do anything to fix it. They have no intention of leaving and just weave their toxic web of drama and gossip."

*I wonder who he's talking about. He's not implying it's me...is he?*

"I used to have an open-door policy, but some people overused it to complain about everyone but themselves. They used to consume a lot of my time. I had to stop being soft spoken and challenge those folks to step up and take action to solve their own problems. Some chose to change, and others needed an experience with a bigger impact before they changed."

Chris paused and leaned forward in his chair.

"I realized that good people have difficulties that I might never know about. I found that I can help circumvent most of the drama by recognizing my superstars early and often. I make the time to show them that they matter. It's my *pay-it-forward* approach."

*"Pay it forward?"*

"It's a combination of walking your talk and investing in others. I've found that good leaders get people to believe in them, but *great* leaders get people to believe in themselves. Nobody is perfect, but people respect you more when your actions and your words align. Now if you'll excuse me, James, I need to make sure I invest the rest of my time here wisely. Do you mind if we pick this up tomorrow?"

"Oh, sorry. Sure thing, Mr. Raven. Good night."

James continued to think about this on the way to his car.

## TWELVE

# The Dynamic Duo
## Meet Zen Ninja

James sprang from the SUV to meet Mason.

"How was your day, bud?"

"It was all right. How about you? Did you have to fight any villains?"

"No villains today. Actually, I met a very special hero today."

"Oh yeah? Tell me, Dad!"

"Well, I had a meeting today with a mysterious person."

"I bet you thought it was going to be a villain after the crazy day you had yesterday, right?"

"Actually, I talked with Mommy last night, and she told me that I shouldn't look for villains right away because I might miss a hero in disguise. I should look for heroes because then I'll find them."

"Like when the sun is in your eyes and it's hard to see?"

"Exactly! See, sometimes, when the sun is in Daddy's eyes, or when I've heard something bad about a person before, I might not give them a fair chance."

"Yeah, and you might try to punch them before they punch you?"

"Kind of. Mommy told me that I should assume positive intent and be curious first. I should see if they know the secret handshake."

"And if they don't, then you know they are a villain?"

"Sometimes Daddy needs to be curious and find out what they stand for."

"Oh, you don't want to fight a hero and let the bad guys get away."

"Exactly, Mason."

"Does assuming positive intent give you x-ray vision?"

"You got it, little buddy!"

Excitedly, Mason asked, "Which hero did you meet today, Dad?"

"Actually, I met with two people who represented the same hero!"

"Huh? Two people were the same hero? Do you mean they were like the Dynamic Duo or the Wonder Twins?"

"No, Mason, they were two different people who shared very similar beliefs and behaviors. They both care about people and relationships. They come from a place of selflessness, cooperation, and teamwork. One was a man, and one was a woman."

"So cool. Two ordinary, everyday people who transform into the same hero…whoa, now that's awesome!"

"I learned that some people are patient, soft spoken, and deliberate," James said. "They seek to maintain a peaceful environment where people and relationships matter. They prefer not to be in the spotlight and instead have a behind-the-scenes approach to leadership."

"What's their superpower?"

"They are supportive, relaxed, and able to keep calm in the chaos. They slice through evil intentions with ninja-like precision."

"Ninjas are subtle and cautious but should never be underestimated! We need to come up with a name for them…"

"Mason, are you thinking what I'm thinking?"

"Yeah!"

They said it together: "Zen Ninja!"

"Sounds like you've heard of them, Mason."

"I've heard stories of their powers and abilities, but you got to experience them in action. You are so lucky! Do you think I can meet them someday?"

"Maybe, Mason. Maybe…"

James and Mason finished their hero conversation, dropped off Mason's things at home, and headed to Chipotle and then to church.

"OK, Mace. I'll see you at eight thirty. I'll pull up in the front circle. Only come out when you see the Team Rizzo transporter, OK?"

"OK, Dad."

Mason took off toward a pack of his friends. They said their good-byes simultaneously.

"Bye!"

"See you later!"

James watched Mason twirl through the revolving door.

*I love that little guy. He never ceases to amaze me. How could he know about Zen Ninja? I wish I had learned these lessons at his age. Heck, I'm pretty happy to be learning them now.*

James drove to the end of the parking lot and tapped out a message to Suzy.

You free? Just taking a few minutes to collect myself.

James tossed his phone on the passenger seat.

"Phew...what a day! All right, what do I need to do now? Hmm."

James scanned the passenger seat and spied his hero notebook.

*I could really use the time to process some of this hero and villain stuff. I'm sure there is a hero habit buried in there somewhere...*

James grabbed his notebook and started journaling. He filled the pages with his thoughts, assumptions, and concerns. Then he stopped and began talking to himself.

"That's it! *Pay it forward!* I found another hero habit! I'd better capture this."

James flipped to a new page and began writing.

*Zen Ninja*

# HERO HABIT
## PAY IT FORWARD

I want to make time for what's most important, but its so hard to determine where to invest my time and energy. It feels like I keep taking one step forward and two steps back, and it's totally DRAINING me!

I want to be successful and help others MAKE A DIFFERENCE, but I keep falling a little short, and it's affecting my confidence, my relationships, and my health.

I know that sometimes work takes priority over relationships, and I also know that too much focus on results can deteriorate TRUST and RESPECT.

PAYING IT FORWARD allows me to build relationship reserves in advance to weather any PERFECT STORM.

My villain is stubborn passive-aggressive and resistant to change. He convinces me to procrastinate under pressure, retreat from conflict, and avoid making tough decisions.

Hero Tip:
Heroes are empathetic, cooperative, and dependable. Typically someone made a significant investment in their lives, and they are committed to repaying this debt.

Heroes invest in life by PAYING IT FORWARD.

James thoughts were interrupted by a text from Suzy.

> I could be available. Are you in a better mood, or are you going to use me as a therapist for another one of your awful days?

*Ouch, I deserve that. You'd better respond with something funny…*

Last night was Supervillain James. This is just plain James. The one who knows the counselor is gone for the night. Kisses.

James rang Suzy.

"Hi, babe."

"James, you know you need help, right?"

"We both know I need help, Suzy, but I'm doing my best with what I have."

"I know we have a lot going on, but last night you made me angry."

"Well, obviously. You hung up on me. That hasn't happened in over ten years!"

"James, I just think that we need to communicate better, or our *want to's* will start to feel like *have to's.*"

"*Want to's feel like have to's?*" he asked.

"Yeah, when all the fun stuff we want to do starts to feel like just another thing we have to do. That's a red flag that we are on a path to destruction."

"A path to destruction? Suzy, it sounds so 'all or nothing.'"

"James, we've both seen it. We can each name a half-dozen couples who started out just like us, and they're already divorced. I don't want to drift further apart by just grinding through the next twelve years. After Mason goes off to college, I don't want to be sitting across the kitchen table, wondering who this stranger is that I'm married to."

"This is pretty heavy stuff, Suzy. What's going on over there?"

"I've had a lot of time to talk to Mom over the past few days. She's told me stories about how this happened to them after my brother died and I moved in with you. Honestly, if it can happen to them, it can happen to us."

"Wow. Suzy, I'm kinda shocked. I thought we were going to reconnect, and now I'm taken aback."

"Sorry, James. I guess I might be the one venting tonight. It's been a tough day. Dad had angioplasty, and he's in pretty rough shape. I've realized that he's not my invincible daddy anymore, and I think it's taking its toll on me."

James and Suzy talked candidly for the next hour.

"James, I know you have a lot going on and want the best for us, but it feels like our world is falling apart. I want things to be the way they were. I'm sorry for being such an emotional basket case. I'm feeling…"

*OK, James, it's time to break out some of those hero skills right about now. You know she is stressed; you know she needs certainty; you know she loves you and wants everything to be back to normal.*

"Suzy, I wish I could turn back time and make everything the way it was the day we recited our vows. I love you! I promise that we won't just get through this together; we will become stronger as a couple and as a family because of it."

James heard Suzy sniffling and beginning to cry.

"Mason and I have been using this experience to bond and convert these life lemons into some of the tastiest lemonade."

Suzy chuckled, and James continued.

"Your Supermen will be there Friday by midnight," he said. "It's just a few more days. What can I do for you until then?"

"Well, can you call me on your way home so I can talk to Mason? I'm struggling without you guys."

"We will do one better: we'll FaceTime you after we leave the church. Keep your phone close, OK?"

"I will. James, thank you and I love you!"

"I love you too!"

## THIRTEEN

# Policy as a Weapon
## Meet Energy Vampira

The morning was off to a good start. James and Mason had a healthy breakfast, traffic was incredibly light, and he even arrived at work fifteen minutes early. As he backed into a stall directly in front of the office, he began to think.

*Today is going to be great! I'm going to meet with a bunch of heroes, and they will provide a perfect perspective. It's going to be a beautiful day…*

James watched as the morning shift began entering the building. *Everyone seems pretty happy. My attitude must be contagious. People are saying hello and holding the door for each other. Maybe they really are a work family. Well, every family has some dysfunctional members. Tsk, tsk, James, don't think like that! Remember, today you're looking for heroes!*

"Morning, Emily. Nice to see you!"

"It's nice to be seen again, James."

"Huh?"

"I was pretty sick yesterday, and I'm just glad to be back to my old self again! Today you will be meeting with a couple managers, a few supervisors, and with Ashley, one of our frontline employees."

*Great! I can't wait. I hope to have another day like yesterday!*

"I have you set up in a conference room for the day. I'll make sure to remind everyone of their time, and I'll check in on you intermittently."

"Thank you, Emily. I'm so glad you are feeling better!"

James pulled some items from his bag and awaited his guests. During the meetings, James was curious. He listened more than he talked while attempting to figure out what winning looked like for each person and each department.

Emily popped in as the last person exited the conference room.

"Perfect timing, Emily! I just finished."

"Great, James. I'll take you to Ashley for your desk-side."

As James followed Emily down the hallway, past the empty cube from last night, he began to think about Ashley.

*Mr. Raven mentioned her results are near the top. I'm excited to learn her approach. I bet she can teach me a lot!*

"Excuse me, Ashley, I'd like to introduce James, who will be joining you for the next hour."

"Thanks, Emily. Hi, James."

"I'm excited to join you today so you can help bring all of this together."

"Whoa, James, let's keep expectations low for today. That way I have a chance of exceeding them."

*Hmm, that's an interesting perspective. I wonder what she means by that. Don't overanalyze her response. Just go with the flow for now…*

Ashley smirked and quickly provided James with a headset similar to the one he had worn the day before, although no additional directions were given.

"All right, James, let's get moving. I'm one of the top producers here, and I didn't get there by chitchatting. Let's jump into our first call."

James sat in shock as Ashley treated the caller like a number, listened only for what she wanted to hear, and interrupted the customer midsentence while using company policy as a weapon to defend her tactics.

*What just happened? Was that for real?*

"Ashley, what was your intention with that customer? What did winning look like for that call?"

"Winning, on that call? Well, it looked like it does on most calls. I needed to make sure to rein in the vastly optimistic requests of the customers and set realistic expectations. Then I needed to make sure they got through the process as quickly as possible so I could get on to the next task in my queue."

James's eyes widened as he tried to control his disbelief.

"See, James?" Ashley pointed to the bottom right of her computer screen at the growing queue of customer contacts.

"I need to get through these calls to make my quota. I'm sure they have you sitting with me because I consistently exceed my daily call quota. That's more than I can say for others around here…"

Ashley rolled her eyes and scanned her peers in both directions.

"James, my manager told me that our results were suffering. He told me to eliminate excuses, focus on the goal, and meet or exceed my daily quota."

"But what about your customers? What about their experience?"

"James, they already lost when they got into that accident or had their car stolen. I'm here to get them a check so they can get back on with their life; I'm not here to help them hit the lottery."

*Jeez, she seems so sarcastic and generalizing. Maybe I'm missing something; maybe I can turn this around with a great question.*

"What do you think they're experiencing as a result of their loss?"

"Honestly, James, between you and me, I can't play therapist to these folks. If I did, I'd end up missing my numbers and be put on a performance-improvement plan. I'd be even more stressed, and it wouldn't do anyone any good."

*She keeps talking about can'ts and won'ts. I'm not getting through...*

"James, although I'd love to chitchat, we need to move on."

Ashley clicked her mouse, and the phone began to ring again.

James sat through several more calls as Ashley continued to treat people like numbers, pushing to get done quickly and achieve her daily metrics.

*Is this what they want from employees here? Metrics at any cost? Maybe Stephanie is the unicorn. Maybe they really want to create an army of Ashleys. It feels like she sucked the energy out of me and every customer too! Can this just be over already?*

"All right, that's the show for today," Ashley said. "I'm sure you have plenty of work to do. I sure do. I hope you got what you were expecting!"

*I sure didn't! I thought this was supposed to be a work family. I thought they were devoted to helping people recover in their moments of need. It seems like Ashley is the opposite of everything Mr. Raven and I discussed yesterday...*

"Thanks, Ashley. Good-bye."

James grabbed his bag and headed toward his car. He passed Mr. Raven's office on the way, but his door was closed, and James noticed a few folks attentively seated in the chairs opposite his desk. He glanced at Emily, but she was on the phone, so he threw her a wave and drove back to headquarters.

*I don't get it. Today was supposed to be a slam dunk. I was looking for heroes, but I think I found another villain. Why is this happening to me? I feel bad for our customers. Ashley missed so many obvious opportunities to delight them and boost their satisfaction. She sucked the last bit of energy from each of them and from me too. She's an energy vampire. No, she's Energy Vampira! Maybe how you achieve your metrics matters less than what metrics you actually achieve. It seems like such a lost opportunity!*

*Energy Vampira*

## FOURTEEN

# Pure Chaos
## A Bigger, Badder Storm

James was confused, struggling to make sense of what he had experienced. Upon entering headquarters, he eyed the elevator and then the stairs.

*I should take the stairs, but I'm just too busy. I need to get to my desk, catch up on e-mails, and figure out what to tell Bob about this morning's meetings.*

James rushed into the open elevator doors and pressed the third-floor button.

*Come on. Come on! Why is this stupid elevator always so slow? I knew I should have taken the stairs!*

As the doors opened, James, trying to make up lost time, collided with Val.

"Oh, James, glad you could join us today," she said sarcastically. "Looks like you conveniently missed our update meeting. I see the Boston project isn't on your priority list!"

"Huh? I shot you an e-mail last night…"

"No, you didn't, or I would've seen it. My client called me in a tizzy right after our scheduled meeting. They grilled me about your portion, and I was unprepared. Seriously, if you're going to blow someone off, at least have the courtesy to tell them in advance so they don't look like an idiot!"

"I'm sorry, Val. I—"

Val abruptly continued. "Sorry won't cut it anymore. It's always someone else's fault. It can't be your fault; you're the golden boy. I'm tired of helping you look good while you position yourself for my promotion. I'd rather do it myself than rely on you anymore!"

The elevator doors began shrieking their high-pitched buzz. Val stomped into the elevator and turned to face James as the doors started to close.

"You're off the Boston project!" she said. "Now you'll have all the time you need for your special project. You certainly won't be sabotaging mine anymore!"

As the doors closed, James shook his head and blinked his eyes.

*Why is she so over the top about this? I sent her an e-mail and proposed a new time to meet. She's so blunt and uncompromising!*

Bob spotted him from down the aisle.

"James, do you have a few minutes?"

"Uh, sure, Bob," James replied, still reeling from his altercation.

"Meet me in my office in two minutes."

Bob continued walking toward the windows, grabbed a few documents off the printer, and headed back to his office. James hung his jacket over the back of his chair and took a deep breath.

*He must have heard Val's tirade. She's a loose cannon and needs to be reined in. I'm sick of dealing with her storming in and creating all sorts of chaos wherever she goes. I'm glad Bob saw that!*

James knocked on Bob's door.

"Come in, James, and have a seat." Bob motioned to one of the empty chairs opposite his desk.

"Hi, Bob. I assume you overheard Val's little tirade?"

"Actually, I just wanted to get an update on your projects. Is the Val thing pertinent to this conversation?"

"Well, kind of. It seems like whatever I do is never enough for her, and she flies off the handle whenever things aren't done exactly the way she wants."

"Val does have a certain way of doing things, but it's been working for her—"

"Yeah, it's called steamrolling. She's controlling, overbearing, and an outright bully. I think someone needs to talk to her about it."

"Are you suggesting I talk to her about it?"

Bob peered at James, seeking clarification.

"No. Well, yeah, I guess."

"James, from what I heard, Val was expecting something for her client update, and you didn't deliver. I'd be pretty upset too."

"I told her I couldn't be there and proposed a new time to meet. It's not my fault!"

"James, I don't care whose fault it is. I know you two will work it out amongst yourselves. You are both capable professionals."

James pursed his lips and bit his tongue.

*Well, at least one of us is. She's a long way from being professional!*

"Seriously, Bob, how long are you going to let her get away with her tirades? She gets all worked up, makes a big scene, and says things that aren't true."

"Says things like what?"

"Like I'm off the Boston project and she can handle it herself. She needs me! I provide a ton of value to the team—"

Bob held up his hand.

"Stop, James. You and Val are a lot alike. You're both smart, outgoing, and determined. You have a ton of talent and great potential, but you both have a few rough edges too."

Bob inched closer to James.

"I need you to listen with wisdom beyond your age right now."

*Is he trying to have a Yoda-and-Luke moment with me? Tell me something he must!*

"Val is determined, demanding, and strong willed," Bob said. "Those are her strengths. That is why we hired her, and that is why she is leading some of our biggest projects with our external clients. Sometimes she focuses so much on the task that she forgets about maintaining relationships. She allows her strengths to reach a tipping point, and they become an opportunity area."

*Ha! Opportunity area? More like a glaring weakness...*

"I'm working with her on her opportunity areas like I'm working with you on not taking challenges and setbacks so personally and on catching yourself when you exaggerate and become sarcastic."

*Me? Sarcastic? I'm not sarcastic!*

"James, you need to realize that you are not perfect! Otherwise you're going to keep learning lessons the hard way."

*The hard way. What does he mean, "the hard way"?*

"I'm going to be transparent. I relate to Val. She is objective in her communications. It's not that she doesn't like people; it's just that her focus is on getting things done and crossing things off her to-do list. It's her style, and sometimes that style can be abrupt and abrasive to some folks who are more focused on relationships."

*I must be one of those relationship guys because I don't get her...*

"Val is not a bad person. She is a go-getter, and her demanding and determined style can easily slip into commanding and blunt. When deadlines, delays, and distractions trigger her sense of urgency, she doesn't realize the impact of her actions on others. It's not that she wants to be a villain."

*Did he just say villain?*

"Now I suggest you take some time to figure out how to approach Val to get back on the Boston team. Do I make myself clear?"

"Yes, Bob…abundantly clear."

James retreated back to his desk with his tail between his legs.

*Another day in this alternate world where a good guy can't catch a break. Val has "opportunity areas," huh? That's an understatement! I guess he just doesn't see it. I can't believe he thinks I'm sarcastic and exaggerate? Pssh!*

James rolled his eyes and then spotted a picture of Suzy and Mason pinned to his cube wall. He smiled and took a deep breath.

*Well, if I'm being honest, Suzy has given me that feedback too. Maybe I just need to assume positive intent and try to make sense of all this craziness…*

*The Storm*

# FIFTEEN

# Heroes versus Villains
## Where Is the Easy Button?

James was stressed and ready to throw in the towel on this hero habits stuff. He just wanted to complain about anyone who had a different perspective from his. Catching up on e-mails, James found his meeting proposal to Val stuck in his outbox. The rest of Friday flashed by as he scrambled to get home, pack for the weekend, and prepare for the flight.

*What is with all of these people being the same crazy way on the same crazy day? Am I the only sane one left?*

James selected a few sets of clothes and placed them into his suitcase. He sighed and shook his head.

*Could it be me? Nah, I'm totally self-aware. Well, when I met Mr. Raven, I did jump the gun and try to prove my worth too soon. Now I know he was just standing up for his people. I thought he was a villain, but maybe I have more to do with this than I thought.*

He reached into his armoire and pulled out a couple pairs of socks.

*OK, maybe with Mr. Raven, but what about Bob? Well, I guess he did come from having lunch with Chris and might have felt partially responsible. Bob typically jumps into action, and maybe he was so focused on fixing the situation that his message got delivered objectively. Actually, if I was in Bob's position, I'd be pretty pissed!*

James zipped the suitcase closed and hoisted it down the stairs.

*I'll think more about that later. I need to pack Mason's bag, tidy up the house, send an e-mail to Val, and...what about Val?*

James stopped in the kitchen and placed both hands on the counter facing the fireplace.

*She and I are nothing alike! I have good intentions, and I'm self-aware! Sure, I slip once in a while, but only when the perfect storm of unexpected challenges crashes all at once.*

James shook his head, thinking about the avalanche of chaos he'd experienced that week.

*If Val had even half of what I have going on right now, her head would explode. She's self-centered, short tempered, and willing to steamroll anyone who gets in her way. Who would ever marry someone like her, anyway?*

A text from Suzy interrupted James's thoughts.

> Hi, babe. What's shakin'? Are you thinking about me or what?

*Thinking about her? Yeah, right. I'm just trying to scrape my life together.*

James plunked down on the couch to take Suzy's call.

"Hi, James. Everything OK over there? How are my boys?"

James looked to the ceiling and began rolling his eyes.

"Hi, Suz. Today's been another one of those days. I'm spent!"

"Again?" Suzy replied emphatically.

"Yeah, again. I think something must be in the water over here."

"What happened to Super Daddy and your hero habits?"

"Today I met the biggest villain yet! She sucked the energy out of me from the start. I tried to *assume positive intent*, and she just broke me down. It's like she knew mental jujitsu. I tried everything, but I was no match for her."

"I think you've lost it, James!"

"I think I'm sane, but maybe not. It just seems like everyone else is flipping from hero to villain every other day. How else can I explain this insanity?"

"James, you must be stressed, because you're thinking in black-and-white terms. When you get like this, the answer is usually some shade of gray."

*Hmm…maybe people aren't either heroes or villains, but they vary between the two. Maybe they are heroes when things are going well and villains when they are stressed. Maybe when they overuse their strengths, they tip into being a villain. Maybe heroes and villains are opposite ends of the same spectrum.*

"Genius! Absolute genius…"

"James, what's going on over there? What's genius?"

"Nothing, Suzy. It's all starting to make sense!"

"James, I'm concerned that you aren't handling being alone with Mason too well. I know it's tough, James, but you've got to pull yourself together…"

"Don't worry, Suzy. I think I finally put the last pieces of the puzzle in place."

"What puzzle?"

"I have to let you go so I can write this down in my notebook."

"Uh, OK, I guess. James, please don't make me regret leaving you alone with Mason."

"Don't worry, Suzy. I'm just a little *crazy*, but it will all be fine.

I'll fill you in when we arrive. It will all make sense then, trust me."

James leaped from the chair, pulled a stack of papers out of his workbag, and tossed them across the counter. He dug out his hero journal and flipped to an empty page...

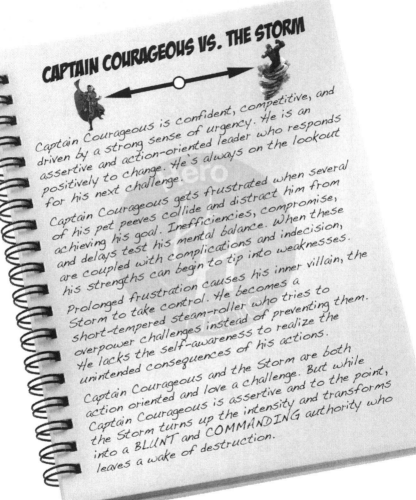

## CAPTAIN COURAGEOUS VS. THE STORM

Captain Courageous is confident, competitive, and driven by a strong sense of urgency. He is an assertive and action-oriented leader who responds positively to change. He's always on the lookout for his next challenge.

Captain Courageous gets frustrated when several of his pet peeves collide and distract him from achieving his goal. Inefficiencies, compromise, and delays test his mental balance. When these are coupled with complications and indecision, his strengths can begin to tip into weaknesses.

Prolonged frustration causes his inner villain, the Storm to take control. He becomes a short-tempered steam-roller who tries to overpower challenges instead of preventing them. He lacks the self-awareness to realize the unintended consequences of his actions.

Captain Courageous and the Storm are both action oriented and love a challenge. But while Captain Courageous is assertive and to the point, the Storm turns up the intensity and transforms into a BLUNT and COMMANDING authority who leaves a wake of destruction.

## SIXTEEN

# A Second Chance
### Hero Habit: Choose Happiness

After arriving late Friday night with Mason, James awoke restless Saturday morning in Suzy's childhood bedroom.

"Suzy, I can't sleep. I'm going in to see Bill. You mentioned meeting me at the hospital after lunch with Mace and Nana, right?"

"Sure, that will give Mason and Nana some time to reconnect. Then we can stop at the grocery store, and I can show Mom some healthier food options."

"Perfect!" James gave Suzy a long kiss and headed to the VA hospital.

As he walked down the sterile hallway lined with gurneys and wheelchairs, the reality of the situation sank in. James stopped at the doorway and gazed into the room where Bill was lying.

Bill, feeling James's presence, turned his head toward the door and opened his eyes wide, exposing his revitalized baby blues.

"James! I'm glad you came. Come, sit with me."

As James sat down, Bill's gown pulled aside, exposing his leg. His veins bulged from his skin, and his frail ankles jutted out. James placed his hand over Bill's as his eyes began to tear. James's heart felt as if it were being ripped from his chest. His once-strong father-in-law was now frail. He had lost thirty-five pounds over the past several months and had become skin and bones.

While James pondered the reality of the situation, Bill broke the silence.

"James, don't ever get old. It sucks!"

*What? How can he be cracking jokes while he's lying here hooked up to these machines?*

"James, I died yesterday, and I saw heaven. My sons greeted me at the pearly gates and told me that it wasn't my time. They said I still have work to do. So I began walking back, and I woke up here." Bill motioned a *ta-da* and pointed to his bed.

"Walking into the light, I was flooded with all of the greatest memories from my life. It was transformational. I realized that when you are here, you can either focus on *those* memories or you can focus on what everybody else is *not* doing or is doing *wrong*... like these guys."

Bill motioned to his veteran roommates, who occupied the other three corners of the room. Then Bill pulled James closer.

"These guys complain about *everything*, all day long."

James smiled and wiped the corners of his eyes.

"James, make sure you have plenty of memories so they can keep you smiling when you end up here. Memories don't just happen; you make them! I'm going to tell you something that took me sixty-eight years to understand. You got your ears on?"

Bill reached up and tried to tune James's ears as he used to do with Suzy.

"There is only one way to make happy memories, and it's my greatest life lesson."

Bill extended his right index finger to the ceiling.

"You need to *choose happiness.*"

*Well, duh. What else are you going to choose? Misery?*

"At some point, we are all going to die. We need to choose how we are going to spend our time between now and then. No matter how many workouts or roundhouse kicks you do, you will end up here, just like me. Remember, happiness comes from the inside. It's a choice; it's something you control. Choosing happiness is simple, but it's not always easy."

"So what's your secret?"

Bill winced and slowly continued. "Life is made of a series of tiny moments. When everything is going well, it's easy to listen to our inner hero, but when stuff happens, the villain sings a sweet song of blame and deflection. It's in those moments that we must choose to believe the hero."

"The hero?"

"Yeah. We have two voices in our head: one is the hero, and the other is the villain. Our job is to determine which voice is which."

James continued the conversation with Bill until the nurses came in to conduct their morning rounds. James watched Bill wince in pain as the nurses helped him off the bed and to the bathroom.

*Someday I hope to be like Bill. Even when he's in pain, he's still looking for the good. He's choosing to be happy regardless of what is happening to him. I think Bill taught me another hero habit!*

While Bill was being evaluated, James took advantage of the time to capture the hero habit in his notebook…

## HERO HABIT
## CHOOSE HAPPINESS

I haven't been seeing too clearly lately. I've allowed my villain to cloud my perspective and take control. He's got my attitude set to MISERY, not HAPPINESS!

When I listen to my inner hero, I shift from being SELFISH to being SELFLESS. I focus more on the mission & objectives than the problems and obstacles.

It's like Maryse says:
"God wraps a gift in a problem, and sometimes we focus so much on the PROBLEM that we forget to open the GIFT!"

Challenges require me to leverage my strengths and dig deep to achieve the goal. When I know and align with my purpose, I create a RIPPLE EFFECT. And when I surround myself with others who are leveraging their strengths, we create the ULTIMATE HERO TEAM.

Hero Tip:
Sometimes it's EASY to choose happiness, and sometimes it feels IMPOSSIBLE, but in either case, I must remember that it is MY CHOICE! Happiness is a mind-set and I choose happiness!

## SEVENTEEN

# The Favor
## Hero Habit: Be Here

After Bill got back to his bed and took several minutes to center himself, he continued the conversation as if it had never ended.

"James, will you do me a favor?"

"Sure, Bill, anything! What do you want?"

"Today I was supposed to help support the children's hospital and take part in a 'Magical Afternoon of Disney' fundraiser, but now I'm here."

"So…you want me to attend a fundraiser for you?"

"Kind of. I usually dress in a costume to inspire the unwell children. It takes less than two hours, and Suzy will understand. Heck, you might even like it."

"Bill, I'm honored, but I'm only here until tomorrow, and—"

"Are you going to deny a dying man his final wish?"

*Did he really go there? Sounds like a setup, but how can I say no?*

"OK, Bill. What do you want me to do?"

"If you hustle, you can be back before the family gets here."

James headed across campus to the children's wing, following

Bill's directions. Exactly two hours later, he returned to Bill's room.

"How was your experience?" Bill squinted to see James's reaction.

James paused, then a big smile broke across his face.

"I got to be Tigger! Some children would run up to me and give me a big Tigger hug, while others would scurry behind their parent's leg. I was hugging everybody, taking pictures with babies and children, parents and nurses. I would pretend to sign Tigger's autograph and hand them my picture. It was a lot of work, but it was *pure joy* and something I will never forget!"

Bill winced and adjusted the IV in the back of his hand.

"Then something amazing happened," James went on. "After an hour, Goofy and I were selected to visit the children who are too sick to leave their rooms."

Bill squeezed out a smile.

"The hospital staff escorted me to the room of a five-year-old girl. It was deathly quiet, with only her mother's whisper and the steady beeping of machines."

James sniffed and wiped the corners of his eyes as he continued.

"She couldn't have been more than forty pounds, with jet-black hair. She was motionless as I approached her bedside. Her tiny hands were strapped with IVs, and a clear tube was coming out of her nose and taped to the side of her face. A bundle of wires shot out from her small pink hospital gown. She looked sad and totally exhausted.

"I reached over the railing and patted her arm. She just stared at me. Then I handed her a stuffed Tigger, and she slowly reached out and took it. I took a picture and held it close to my Tigger heart and handed it to her."

James pressed lightly onto Bill's chest to convey his touch.

"My heart broke as she strained to accept my gift, so I just laid it beside her. I felt helpless and didn't know what to do, so I placed my big Tigger paws over my eyes and removed them quickly. She smiled, and I could see her incredibly beautiful brown eyes. Then, ever so slowly, she moved her hands over her eyes, pulled them away, and whispered, 'Boo.'"

James swallowed hard as tears rolled down his cheeks.

"Bill, I was a wreck inside that steamy Tigger head, but I jumped back to make her believe that she had scared me. She beamed with the cutest smile. Then I felt her mother's hand on my back.

"Her mother said, 'I know that there is someone inside this costume, and while I may never know who you are, I want you to know that this is the first time that my baby has smiled in over three months. *Thank you* for being here.'

"I nodded and gave her a double Tigger thumbs-up. She watched for what seemed like an eternity as her daughter forgot all the reasons that kept her imprisoned in that hospital bed."

Bill squeezed out a partial smile. "James, I never know what is going to happen, but I do know that my small effort can make a huge difference in someone's life. Especially when that someone is a helpless little child dealing with such insurmountable pain."

"Thank you, Bill."

"James, service is the cure to selfishness…and that service could be one of your end-of-life moments—a moment you remember when you're old and gray and end up in this room."

James nodded, with tears still rolling down his cheeks.

"The important thing is to understand *why* this moment touched you so deeply and *how* you made it happen…because this was all you, James."

"Bill, I *never* would have done it without you forcing me to do it."

"Sure, James. Sometimes we all need someone to push us beyond our comfort zone, but it was *you* who were totally present for those kids. You made the choice to eliminate excuses and distractions and just *be there* for those kids. You'll never know the full impact of your actions, but guys like us feel an obligation to give back in a meaningful way. It's in our DNA. It's who we are and what we do."

"Suzy told me you do it because of the ripple effect it creates. You told her the benefits far outweigh the sacrifices."

"James, you are a good student and can sometimes be a great listener, but Suzy let me in on a little secret. She told me that you guys have been having trouble communicating recently."

James's eyes shot up from the bed and met Bill's.

"James, I know a little bit about being an energy vampire myself."

"She told you I've been an energy vampire?"

"Not in those words, James, but you and I are a lot alike. I know that we are both outgoing, dynamic, and persuasive most of the time. We get our energy from others, and when we don't, our positivity and optimism can quickly turn into negativity and pessimism. Instead of building people up and recognizing the good in life, we can tear people down and find everything that is wrong."

"I just discovered Energy Vampira in one of my clients."

"James, it's easy to see in others what we need to fix in ourselves. It's easier to point our finger at others than it is to look at ourselves in the mirror."

"I get it, Bill. I know I have been on the fritz lately, trying to do too much and not asking for help. I've been slipping and have been becoming someone else in the process. I'm not proud of it."

"That's great! The first step is awareness. Now you need to do something about it! I'm not here to beat you up. You're doing a great job of that already."

A hearty laugh broke the tension of their conversation.

"Just twenty minutes ago, you had an incredible experience because you were fully present for someone other than yourself. You made that child's day and her mother's, too. You did it because you chose to be present. You chose to take action. You chose to *be here*… in that moment…to make a difference."

"I had a lot of assumptions and judgments about your request."

"James, your assumptions are blind spots, and they are hindering your ability to *be here* in the critical moments of your life. They are clouding your vision and keeping you from seeing the good in people. I think you are assuming negative intent."

"How did you learn about the hero habits?"

"Hero habits?"

"Yeah, about energy vampires and the hero habits."

"James, you need to find a way to stop allowing your assumptions to dominate your world. Being confident is one thing, but not being aware of your biases and assumptions will cost you much more than a job, title, or promotion."

Bill winced as he pulled James's hand closer.

"You and I are very similar, James. That is why I gave you Suzy's hand in marriage. That is why it is easy for me to see your struggles so clearly. I learned about energy vampires and about *being here* the hard way. I almost lost everything, and now I have a second chance. I want to give you that same wake-up call before you lose all that is good in your life."

Their moment was interrupted as Mason yelled, "*Papa!*" and raced across the room and began squeezing and kissing Bill's hand. After absorbing the emotion of their reunion, James stepped out and captured Bill's advice in his notebook.

*Bill and I are more similar than I thought! I get it. This is my wake-up call. I never want to forget this moment or the lessons Bill taught me. I'd better capture these now so I can be here for my family… because they are what matters most of all!*

*Energy Vampire*

# HERO HABIT
# BE HERE

I wouldn't have believed that dressing up like Tigger for a couple hours would have me feeling so INSPIRED! Seeing that little girl really put my life in perspective. My struggles are NOTHING to the pain she endures every day.

I'm so blessed to have been able to visit those kids! I know that when I'm PRESENT, I ask great questions and I see opportunities that I otherwise might have missed. I'm able to see the good in others and take a moment to RECOGNIZE them for going above and beyond!

My villain sets traps to distract me. He entices me to check my phone during meetings and to be thinking about being somewhere else. He pushes people away by BLAMING them and shirking RESPONSIBILITY, creating a SPIRAL of NEGATIVITY, but my hero knows that it takes a TEAM to make the IMPOSSIBLE become a REALITY!

Hero Tip:
When I'm PRESENT, I MAKE good things happen. I become an ENCOURAGER, a CHEERLEADER and the person who sparks INSPIRATION in others.

I must BE HERE to BE the HERO!

## EIGHTEEN

# Getting Committed
## Hero Habit: Be All In

Saturday and Sunday were the best and longest of James's life. He was present, aware, and purposeful. On a sunset walk, James and Suzy discussed the hero habits while Nana and Mason played on the swings across the playground. When James turned to walk backward so he could maintain eye contact with Suzy, she started to believe that the old James was back.

"Suzy, when that woman told me her little girl hadn't smiled in months, it crushed me and humbled me at the same time. We have so much good happening in our life. I want to make sure we are *designing a winnable game*. I want to start *assuming positive intent* and *choosing happiness again*. I'm 100% committed!"

Their conversation continued, and they decided that Suzy would keep Mason for a few days so he could spend time with Papa and finish their chess game. James would have a few days to begin applying the hero habits before they arrived home.

On Monday, after taking the red-eye flight, James went straight into Bob's office.

"Bob," he said, "I've been selfish, and I want to apologize. I've been trying to do it all myself, and I've pushed away the people who matter most. I got a second chance with Bill, and I'm taking that perspective into my entire life. Will you please give me a second chance too?"

"James, just when you think you can't give any more, you'll find that if your *why* is big enough, you will always find another level. Remember, committing to change is easy, but following through on your commitment defines your *character*. I think you are ready to hear this."

Bob looked down at his desk, took a deep breath, and began to share his story.

"It was the morning of September eleventh. I'll never forget that day. I was in my office sipping coffee and reviewing the weekly dashboard when Chris Raven burst into my office and told me that Terry needed to see us ASAP."

"Within minutes, I, Chris, and all our peers were sitting around the executive conference table.

"Terry said, 'I'm going to be transparent. None of us have been here before, and I don't know exactly what to do, but we need to know where every single person in our company is *right now!* I don't want anyone in motion. Tell every single person to hunker down and stay where they are, because right now no transportation is safe!'

"James, this was no small task! We had over two-hundred folks dispersed across Manhattan, New York, DC, and Pennsylvania, in all the places where the attacks were occurring.

"Then Terry gave us this mandate: 'I want to know that every person is safe and accounted for! I want you to use whatever means necessary to locate them! You have one hour to find and confirm that every single employee of this company is OK. I want to know if they are sick, on vacation, or in the bathroom. I want to ensure that everyone is *safe!* Is that understood?'

"Everyone nodded their heads emphatically.

"Then Terry said, 'Just as important, I want to make sure they know that their families, spouses, and kids are safe too. We need to know, and they need to know! If that means they need to leave work, pick up kids from school, or contact them by phone, then so be it. Whatever it takes.'

"Listen, James, we were *busy.* This was our peak season. Customers wanted their orders immediately. We had to take people off the production line. Some of my peers were not happy with Terry's decision, but he had to make that call.

"One VP exclaimed, 'What about the orders? We can't abandon our customers!'

"Terry replied, 'Either these events will stop the world, or we'll figure it out later. I'll take the heat for this! Each moment that we don't make a decision could mean someone's life. If we can save even one of our people from being harmed, all of this will be worth it. If we don't act with urgency, we will never be able to forgive ourselves. Revenue, orders, commerce…nothing matters more in this moment! Are you *all in?*'

"Terry made each of us commit to being *all in* before we left the room. That next hour felt like twenty hours, and yet it happened in the blink of an eye. Less than sixty minutes later, we were back in that room with every employee accounted for."

Bob paused and took a few extra seconds to transition from his flashback to become present with James.

"In that moment I learned what it meant to *be all in.* I watched Terry be committed, determined, and outcome focused. His lesson allows me to stand true to my word and be accountable when my *intentions* don't match my *results*. It allows me to understand the impact of my actions and my decisions. It allows me to understand how modeling confident and authentic leadership gives other people the certainty they need to be brave in the tough times, to pledge their loyalty, to commit, and to *be all in*."

James hung on Bob's every word as he remembered his own 9/11 experience. *What's happening? This can't be true. Was that a replay? Oh no…a second plane? This is terrible! Are we at war? What can I do? I can't sit here! I have to do something. I feel so helpless… helpless. Where is Suzy? Is she OK? I have to talk to her right away.*

"Depending on your perspective, many heroes and villains were made on 9/11. At the end of the day, 9/11 forced each of us to take a step back and remember what is *really* most important."

James nodded along.

"Those memories are seared into our brains, and they remind us of what we stand for at our core," Bob said. "Each of us made a commitment that day, based on our beliefs, to get back to who we are at our core. Every time you remember that day, you'll remember the commitment you made. Heroes never lose sight of who they are at their core! They know people need certainty during moments of truth, and they are direct, to the point, and transparent. They provide *certainty* to help others move forward.

"Now you'll need to excuse me, James. Would you mind seeing yourself out?"

James bolted back to his desk and captured his thoughts.

*We each made a different meaning from 9/11. Bob learned what it meant to be all in. I think he taught me another hero habit…*

*Captain Courageous*

## HERO HABIT
## BE ALL IN

Excuses don't matter when I'm ALL IN! I feel CONFIDENT to share my perspective, and I'm CURIOUS to discover the thoughts and ideas of others. This allows me to get a holistic picture so I can commit to the STRATEGIC FIRST ACTIONS required for success.

It's about taking 100% RESPONSIBILITY for my actions and being 100% ACCOUNTABLE for my results regardless of the circumstances. When I'm COMMITTED to overcoming obstacles, delivering the mission, and achieving the GOAL, I allow GREAT things happen!

But when I take things personally and expect others to be more responsible than I am, I allow my inner villain to THRIVE. He is an uncompromising steamroller with a short fuse. He's quick to JUMP TO CONCLUSIONS, he hates distractions & delays, and wants TOTAL CONTROL!

Hero Tip:
Heroes are courageous leaders willing to enter uncharted territory. They are confident, quick to challenge assumptions, and determined to ACHIEVE THE GOAL!

Heroes know GREAT results require them to BE ALL IN.

## NINETEEN

# Hitting Bottom
## I'm My Worst Enemy

After closing up from his marathon day, James returned to his empty house. He attempted to eat the leftover sandwich from lunch, but after the first bite, something happened.

*My stomach doesn't feel well. I think I need to rest for a minute.*

James laid on the couch, pressing his stomach, trying to find relief.

*Whew, taking the red-eye flight this morning really messed me up. I'll just close my eyes for a few minutes and take a little power nap. Then I'll hit the ground running when I wake up.*

James fell into a restless sleep for the next several hours until he was awoken with a stabbing feeling deep in his gut. Then his stomach made an awkward sound, as if water were rushing from one part of his intestines to another.

*I don't feel good. Maybe if I just turn on my side, that will help…*

Immediately, James scrambled off the couch and crawled into the bathroom. He had barely positioned his head over the toilet before he vomited forcefully.

"Ugh. Uggghhhhhh…"

He gasped for air and began wiping the chunky liquid from his chin with a used and foul-smelling washcloth.

*Why is this happening to me? Was it the turkey sandwich from lunch? Or maybe I caught something from that woman next to me on the flight who kept sneezing on me.*

He dry heaved several more times until his head and arms hung lifeless over the toilet bowl.

*Why me? Why now? I just want to stop throwing up. Maybe if I can just get in the shower, then I'll feel better.*

James squirmed out of his splattered clothes and tried to turn on the shower.

*I hope I don't throw up again. God, please save me. I'll do anything!*

James curled into a ball in the tub and sipped the water streaming onto his face, attempting to rid the wretched bile taste from his mouth.

*I'm sure Val has never dealt with a perfect storm like this! Her life must just be a cakewalk. If she had to deal with what I am dealing with this week, she would tap out.*

*Stop it, James. What are you doing? This isn't about Val.*

His temples throbbed with each heartbeat.

*God, I know I've been falling away from you and becoming someone I'm not. I know that I've been judging and blaming Val, Chris, Bob, and the doctor. I keep focusing on what I don't want. I keep pointing out the flaws and mistakes in others when I'm really hiding from who you intended me to be. Please help me! I'll do anything...*

A sudden calm fell over James. He reached up and turned off the shower. Then he dragged himself out of the bathtub and pulled a towel from the bar.

*Thank you! Thank you. If I can just make it to the bed, maybe I can sleep it off. I hope that was the last of it.*

James struggled as his body began to cramp and shiver from the chills. His legs ached, and his head throbbed.

*I've been such a jerk. It's easy to tear down others, but in the end, I feel worse. I take my frustrations out on Suzy and Mason and anyone else who is close to me. I've been taking the easy way out.*

*Stupid hero habits aren't doing me any good right now! Who needs them? Wait, that's it. James, you are such an ungrateful jerk!*

James had hit bottom. His thoughts paused as he stared into the green hue of the clock. The time—3:44 a.m.—shone brightly. His eyes widened, and his throbbing head lifted for a few seconds.

*Is this a foreshadowing of my life? I don't want to die old and alone. I talk a good game about putting family first, but when it comes down to it, I take them for granted. I get lost in my phone and in my work e-mail when I'm supposed to be with them. I'm my own worst enemy...I'm the supervillain!*

James pressed hard against his temples, trying to release the building pressure.

*When am I going to realize that it's my choice to be a hero or a villain? How could I have been so stupid? Oops, there I go again. I'm punishing myself for not being a better dad, husband, and leader. That is my inner villain, and I need to turn down his volume and turn up the volume of my inner hero. OK, what is my hero trying to tell me right now?*

James closed his eyes, relaxed his jaw, and sank into the pillow.

*Close your eyes, take a deep breath, and let me take care of you. Just rest...*

James's forehead started to relax, and he even cracked a smile. He awoke that afternoon feeling sore, exhausted, and alone, but above all else, he felt *alive!*

*Ugh, I'm feeling ten times better than I did last night, but I still feel terrible. I hope I can drink and eat something to get rid of this headache. I wish Suzy was here to take care of me and bring me a banana and maybe some ginger ale. She does so much for our family, and now with Bill's stroke…Suzy and Mason need me more than ever, and I've been so selfish! I don't deserve her. How can I expect them to stay with me if I don't change my habits?*

James sat on the edge of his bed and wiped his hands up and down his cheeks and forehead.

*If I'm being honest with myself, I take my stress out on everyone else. I blame and criticize them, and I deflect my own judgments onto them. When someone points out one of my blind spots, I dismiss their feedback and make that person out to be the villain, but I'm the biggest villain of them all! It's not Suzy, Bob, Chris, Val, or the doctor. It's me. I'm the one who needs to change, not them!*

*So what are you waiting for? This is your life! This is your reality check! Remember that frail little girl in the hospital and the hundreds of sick children? You don't have it so bad. Suck it, up big boy. It's time to be all in!*

*You've got no excuse! Sure, you look like crap and smell terrible, but it's in these moments that heroes are made. In this moment you can choose comfort and familiarity, or you can choose to step into fear and uncertainty. You can choose courage, or you can choose fear. This is a defining moment, one in which heroes do the impossible and find a way to choose happiness!*

"The choice is up to me. I can choose to be a hero or to be a villain. I need to choose who I want to be. And I choose to be the *hero!*"

## TWENTY

# Rebirth of a Hero
## Rising from the Ashes

*feel a thousand times better! I mean, I'm probably only operating at 70 percent, but it's so much better than just a few hours ago. It's a new day. I'm ready to design a winnable game! I'm ready to be here and be present so I can be all in, and in the end, I know it's up to me to choose happiness!*

The next morning, James sprang out of bed, prepared himself for work, and headed into the office.

*How could I have been such a fool? I've been drifting away from who I am, and I've been becoming someone I'm not. I'm trying to do it all myself, and I'm stressed out. I'm eating junk food as a way to cope, and it's killing me! I've been pushing away the people I love most, and I'm aching on the inside. I know what I need to do.*

James dropped his bag at his desk and walked toward Bob's office.

"Well, James, so nice of you to join us today," a voice remarked from behind him.

"I'm glad to be here! Oh, hi, Val."

James looked from Val to Bob's office and then back to Val again.

"Val, do you have a quick minute? I want to talk to you about something. Actually, I want to apologize for how I have been acting lately."

Stung with surprise, Val replied, "I guess—if you make it quick!"

"I've realized that I've been quite a jerk lately to several people, including you. I'm sorry for being caught up in my own little world, for not following through on my commitment to you and the team, and for being so disconnected lately."

"How do I know this isn't another one of your games?"

"In all transparency, Suzy's dad had a seizure ten days ago, and she had to fly out to visit him. He was dead for a few minutes, but we got a second chance with him this past weekend."

"That's terrible."

"While Suzy's been gone, I've been struggling to balance all of my responsibilities. The wheels came off the tracks last week. I thought I sent you a request to change our meeting, and I found it stuck in my outbox. Thirty hours ago, I couldn't even lift my head out of the toilet. I want to apologize and ask if we can start over."

Val stared at James and then dropped her eyes to the floor.

"My husband lost his job six months ago. I've been the sole breadwinner, and I've been trying to be Superwoman. Some days are good, and others feel like the world is working against me. I don't think I have been that nice to you either."

"It sounds like we have more in common than I ever would have believed!

"Last week Suzy taught me a hero habit: *assume positive intent*. I've been trying to apply it, but I've been stumbling quite a bit lately, especially with you."

"James, I'll make you a deal. I'll tell you if you start acting like a jerk again, OK?"

"Sure, Val. That sounds good. Do I get to do the same?"

"Let's not push it, James."

They both laughed, and James continued toward Bob's office, where he knocked on the door.

"Come in." Bob nodded and waved James into his office.

"I just had an enlightening conversation with Val," James told him.

"Enlightening, huh? Tell me more."

"Well, I got to thinking about *being all in*. Thirty hours ago I hit bottom. I had the stomach flu and realized that I couldn't keep blaming everyone else and expecting them to change. I realized that it's *me* who needs to change!"

Bob nodded. "Go on. I'm following you!"

"I seized an opportunity this morning and apologized to Val. I found out that we have been experiencing very similar things in our personal lives. I realized that she is doing the best she can with the cards she's been dealt, too!"

"I'm glad you're feeling better and are starting to see the good in Val."

"Val and I must be so similar that we know how to push each other's buttons. I think I can learn a lot from her, and we can become great allies!"

"James, I'm glad to hear you talking like that again," Bob said. "That's the James I hired and the guy we need around here! Welcome back."

"I'm glad to be back." James smiled and turned to leave the room.

Bob stopped him and asked, "How is Bill doing?"

James shared the news of Bill's recovery and his plans to pick up the family from the airport that night. Then he headed to his desk.

*I hope this morning's events are foreshadowing what's to come. I feel great! Bill is doing better. Suzy, Mason, and Nana are bonding. I'm working things out with Val and Bob. Things are looking up. I'm starting to feel like a hero again!*

James put in his earbuds and began refining his thoughts for the conversation with Mr. Raven the next day.

# TWENTY-ONE

# Déjà Vu
## Hero Habit: Consult the Owl

J ames drove down the winding frontage road to meet with Mr. Raven and discuss the next steps for the call center and James's ongoing role.

Upon entering the building, he said, "Hi, Emily."

"Good morning, James. You are looking awfully chipper today. What's up?"

"Just a great day to be *alive*."

"It sure is. Mr. Raven is expecting you. Follow me."

"Emily, if you don't mind, I'd like to head down there myself."

"Sure, James, that will save me a trip past the doughnuts in the kitchen. I'm trying to eat healthy nowadays."

James paused before knocking on Chris's door.

*It seems like months ago that I was here for the first time. I've learned so much. It's hard to believe it's only been ten days since I jumped the gun in my initial conversation. I need to be transparent with him.*

James's thoughts were interrupted when Chris's voice rang through the door.

"Having some trouble out there, James? Come on in."

James opened the door and they shook hands.

"Chris, I want to apologize for our first meeting. I was unprofessional and clumsy. I feel terrible for how I must have come across."

"Listen, son, I forgave you right after it happened, but you might still need to let it go before it drags you down too much further."

"You're right. Thank you! I've had some things happen in my life recently that have caused me to be a little off. I've taken our last several conversations to heart, and I want to partner with you on this project."

James shared his thoughts and asked Chris to support a six-month on-boarding for new employees, a new leader-development class, and the creation of a culture team to uncover employees' ideas for improvement.

"James, taking a graduated approach is the best possible scenario for everyone involved. I think this pilot program will help our people metabolize the recent changes and allow us to double down on our strategy."

"Chris, I've got to mention that Bob shared the 9/11 story and the impact it had on you both. I really took the '*be all in*' message to heart. It's helped me prioritize what's most important and to recommit both personally and professionally."

"*Be all in?*"

"Bob told me about when your boss pulled you both into the conference room on the morning of 9/11. About how he was transparent and told you that he didn't know exactly what to do or how to do it, but he needed your 100% commitment to get everyone home safely."

Chris nodded.

"That is true, James, but making wrong assumptions can create unintended consequences and drama."

"What do you mean?"

"Well, Bob and I may have been in the same room, but what we experienced highlights the diversity of our perspective.

"It was the morning of September eleventh. I remember like it was yesterday.

"We were right in the middle of peak season. I was reviewing numbers and giving Terry an update when one of my managers popped his head into the office and said, 'Just giving you a heads-up. A small commuter plane crashed into the World Trade Center.' And he left the room. We didn't think much of it until fifteen minutes later, when he came back and told us a second plane had hit the other tower and it might be a terrorist attack.

"Terry turned on the radio, and our worst fears became real. He asked me to close the door, which was always open. He walked over to the bookshelf, plucked a crystal owl from its perch, and lowered himself onto the couch opposite his desk. He began rolling the crystal owl between his fingers. Then he stopped and stared into its eyes. In that moment, I saw Terry *consult the owl*.

"He asked himself, 'OK, what are you going to do? People are dead, the towers are falling, and I'm completely off balance. I can't be off balance right now. I need to make sure everyone is safe.'

"Then he told me to assemble our team ASAP!

"Within ten minutes, me, Bob, and all our peers were sitting around the conference table.

"Terry told us, 'None of us have been here before, but we have the smartest minds in the company sitting around this table. We need to figure out how to make sure every single person is safe and accounted for under our watch.'

"I watched Terry step back and *consult the owl*, and that is the life lesson I took forward and still remember today. Before any big decision, I make time to *consult the owl*, and if possible, I take the evening to process my decision. I attempt to think through the ripple effect of my decision and determine any unintended consequences that it might cause.

"In the past, I've made hasty decisions and hurt innocent bystanders with the unintended consequences of my actions."

Chris spun around in his chair and snatched his own crystal owl from its perch on his bookshelf.

"In that moment, I vowed that I would put people first in my decisions whenever possible. I've consulted the owl in all of my major decisions since that time. When you came in here pushing to disrupt our office harmony, I might have let my stubbornness consume me."

James nodded as if accepting Chris's apology.

"People are the heart of our organization. They are what our customers see as Restoration Insurance. They are how we achieve our goals, and they determine our success. Our people have families and responsibilities far beyond these walls."

"I understand," James said. "You *consult the owl* to make better decisions."

"You got it, James. We don't want to create any needless drama. We know the normal everyday challenges around here will create enough drama. This place isn't just a *job*. We care about each other like family. A work family!"

"You care for them, and they care for you. They give more than they would somewhere else because you have their back."

"Absolutely! Our actions reflect our values, and in every decision we make, we either strengthen or weaken our culture."

Chris squinted and looked toward the ceiling.

"I had a woman from customer service come up to my office the Wednesday after 9/11," Chris said. "With tears streaming down her face, she said, 'You let me go home and take care of my three-year-old daughter. I was scared, she was scared, and all I wanted was to make sure she was safe. She means the world to me, and it meant the world to be there for her in that moment. I'd work for you for *free*.'"

Chris rolled the owl in his fingers as he thought about the many decisions he'd made since 9/11 by consulting the owl.

"James, I want you to have this. It's served me well, and I think it will provide you wisdom beyond your years."

Chris placed the crystal owl in James's outstretched hand.

"Give her a good home."

The next ninety minutes flew by as James and Chris laid out the objectives, set the timeline, and selected the culture team. They parted ways until their next biweekly project meeting. James stopped to check in with Stephanie and Ashley to see if they would want to be on the culture team, and both said yes.

*I'm living the dream. Things are coming together, and I'm enjoying work again. I'm done trying to be someone else. I gotta be me! Otherwise, I get stressed, and my villain creates drama and chaos. When I pause to consult the owl, I can see things that I might have missed and understand how to avoid mistakes, errors, and misunderstandings. Chris just taught me another hero habit!*

James paused in the empty cube to capture his thoughts...

## HERO HABIT
## CONSULT THE OWL

I've been pushing pretty hard lately, and my decisions are creating some unintended consequences. I need to step back and evaluate whether where I'm headed is where I want to go.

I think the owl would tell me that my assumptions are creating a pattern that I'm not able to see on my own. My assumptions keep tripping me up and biasing me in ways I don't even realize. I thought I was self-aware, but I guess I still have room for improvement.

I know I need to make a change, but my villain keeps telling me that it's everyone else's fault. He expects others to read my mind. He's SECRETIVE and SKEPTICAL and basks in ISOLATION. He is a perfectionistic faultfinder who pokes holes in any idea that isn't his.

Hero Tip:
Heroes know that their decisions create a ripple effect and they want to think through all scenarios to reduce risk and eliminate unintended consequences. They help the team PAUSE before making critical decisions, so they don't suffer a foolish mistake.

Heroes make time to CONSULT the OWL.

## MY HERO HABIT

I want to BE THE HERO, but where do I start?

Which hero habit do I need to focus on first?

Of course I need to consult the owl and slow down long enough to see if I'm headed in the right direction, but what if I'm not? What if I need to course correct and make some significant changes?

I'm on the fast track, but to where? What does winning looks like for me now?

I need to start by DESIGNING a WINNABLE GAME!

I know what I WANTED when I graduated, and I learned what I DON'T WANT, but I haven't spent much time thinking about what I DO WANT. Is that weird? Well, it's true...

I want to be a part of a HERO team! A team that leverages their strengths of each member and achieves more than any group of individuals could.

Which hero habit do YOU need to focus on first?

MY HERO HABIT: _____

## TWENTY-TWO

# Welcome Home
## Turning the Page

James packed his belongings and headed to the airport.

*It feels like forever since I've seen Suzy and Mason. I hope they arrive safely! I can't wait to share the new hero habits and show them that I can metabolize all of this change and all of these challenges. Oh, there they are...*

"Hi, love! And there's my big boy!"

James squeezed Suzy, planting an extended kiss on her lips, and then turned to Mason for a high five and a hero hug.

"I missed you two! How was the flight?" James asked.

"Everything was great, and I even got my wings," Mason said.

Mason pulled at a pin on his shirt that reflected his junior pilot status.

"It's great to be home, and I'm even better knowing Dad is recovering too," Suzy said. "I never thought he could have such bad health at sixty-eight, but I guess that's what happens when you stop working out and don't eat right."

James smiled at Suzy and gave her a wink.

"James, are you flirting with me?"

"You bet! Sometimes you don't know what you've got till it's gone. I think we both got a second chance these past two weeks. Being away from you has been quite the experience. I'm glad to say that I've grown a lot since you've been gone."

"Me too! I appreciate my dad even more now. His seizure really helped me put things in perspective. I've been so caught up in the minutiae of our daily life that I started sweating the small stuff. I could have never imagined stepping away for two weeks, but *we* made it happen. Now, let's see if the house is still standing."

James rolled his eyes.

"You don't have to believe me," he said, "but after being sick and having that hitting-bottom experience, I knew that I was capable of far more than I thought. I just needed to start acting in alignment with my priorities. I realized that, without my health and you two, nothing else matters!"

Suzy gave James's hand a squeeze and snuggled into his shoulder.

James continued. "I've been so focused on work that I lost sight of the habits that made me successful. I stopped working out. I stopped engaging in my hobbies. I got lax about what I've been eating, I've tried to do too much on my own, and I haven't leveraged my team. I've been setting myself up for failure. I see it clearly now, but I couldn't see it when I was up to my neck in it!"

"Dad?" Mason spoke up from the back of the SUV.

"Yes, Mason?"

"I beat Papa in chess!"

"No way. You beat Papa?"

"Yep, I told him how much you and I practiced when we first got back from Christmas. Do you think we could start playing again? I really miss playing chess with you."

James nodded, remembering the precious conversations they'd

had during their matches.

"I'd love that. Daddy won't be too busy to play anymore. I'm committed to *being here* with you and Mom. To having more fun times and creating great memories to share with Papa, Nana, and your other grandparents too!"

The ride home was filled with stories, laughter, and smiles.

## TWENTY-THREE

# My Fearless Uncle Carl
## The Power of Belief

James and Suzy put Mason to bed and for the next several hours shared the intimate details of their weeks. They laughed, smiled, and cried together for the first time in almost three years. James shared the remaining hero habits with Suzy until they were interrupted by Mason, who came out of his room crying.

"Suz, let me take care of this. What's wrong, buddy?"

"I had a nightmare. I was lost in the airport on my way home from Papa's, and I couldn't find you or Mom. I was super scared."

James squatted next to Mason and whispered in his ear.

"Don't worry, Mason. You're home, and I'll always be here for you!"

"Dad, can you tell me a story?"

"Sure." James ushered Mason to his bed and crouched down.

"When I was six years old, I was slow, I was clumsy, and I was always the last one picked on the schoolyard playground. I dreamed of being the first kid picked. I dreamed of being the fastest kid in school. I dreamed of being a *superhero*.

"I remember that day. It was one of the last days of school. All the kids were on the playground playing cool versions of tag, like freeze tag and TV tag, but I was standing on the curb kicking wood chips back into the playground. And then I heard the rumble of pipes coming up the street, and as the figure on the motorcycle got closer, I could see it was my fearless Uncle Carl."

Mason's eyes widened momentarily before becoming heavy again.

"I ran to meet him, tripped, and skidded across the wood chips, but before I could cry, my fearless Uncle Carl was there to scoop me up in one arm. He set me down on that splintered wood bench and began tending to my road rash. He didn't care that I was slow and clumsy. He just loved me for being me.

"Now, I didn't get to spend much time with Uncle Carl, so with the tears running down my cheeks, I wrapped my arms around him and squeezed him as hard as I could."

James squeezed Mason and whispered in his ear.

"He said, 'James, I have a surprise for you. It's what you've always wanted.'

"When I opened my eyes, he held out a white box with a purple bow.

"He told me, 'Go ahead; open it!'

"I ripped off that bow and tore open the box, exposing metallic purple fabric with the black Batman logo on it.

"Before I could say a word, he spun me around and tied the black velvet straps around my neck.

"He said, 'This is Batman's cape, and whenever you wear it, you'll be able to run faster, jump higher and you can even *fly*.'

"Then he swatted my butt and said, 'Go give it a try!'

"I bolted across the grass, zipped around the swings, and hurdled that same concrete curb that had tripped me earlier. Then I dove into his arms again."

James dove into Mason's arms and held him tightly as he continued.

"Uncle Carl told me, 'James, this cape doesn't just give you Batman's powers. It gives you all the powers of all your favorite superheroes.'

"I shouted, '*Superhero* powers for *life!*'"

James thrust his fists in the air, assuming his victory pose.

"Whenever I wore the cape, I felt different. I felt stronger, I felt faster, and I believed there was nothing I couldn't do with that cape around my neck!

"I never took that cape off for the rest of the summer. I played in that cape, I ate in that cape, I slept in that cape, and Grandma told me that I even took a bath in that cape!"

"*Dad*, you can't wear clothes in the bath!" Mason exclaimed with a yawn.

"And at the end of the summer, just before school started again, I got to spend the entire day with Uncle Carl. As I sat on his lap, I proudly wore that dirty, tattered, and sun-bleached cape around my neck and told him the stories of the many adventures that my cape had seen me through."

Mason's eyes fluttered as he strained to listen to his father's story.

"I told him about how kids tried to chase me, but I was too fast. About how I was able to fly off the top of the jungle gym without even getting hurt.

"He waited for me to finish. Then he put his finger over my lips and said—"

James placed his index finger over Mason's lips too.

"'James, I have bad news.'

"I looked up into his eyes and said, 'Bad news?'

"'Your cape doesn't have any superpowers. You ran faster, jumped higher, and flew off the jungle gym because you *believed* you could, not because of that cape!'

"I yelled, '*No!* This cape *does* have superpowers! I couldn't have jumped that far or run that fast by myself.'"

James, remembering his disappointment, dropped his eyes to the floor.

"Deep inside, I didn't want to believe I was just a slow, average, husky boy again. Then Uncle Carl lifted my chin and tapped his index finger over my heart and continued.

"'James, there are two people who do battle inside of you each day.'"

Mason's eyes suddenly grew wide.

"'One of them is your inner hero. He believes that you can run faster, jump higher, and that you can even fly! He believes that you *are* good enough and that you *can* make a difference. He believes that you should try your *very* best even when it feels like your best isn't good enough.'

"I sniffled and raised my eyes to his and asked, 'Who is the other person?'

"He explained, 'The other person is a villain. He believes that you are *husky*, *slow*, and *weak*. He believes that you should only look out for yourself. He believes that no one deserves your best and that you shouldn't even try.'

"I looked deep into Uncle Carl's sky-blue eyes and asked, 'Well, who *wins?*'

"And Uncle Carl said, 'Whichever one you *believe.* You can do *anything* you can imagine if you *choose* to listen to your inner *hero.*'"

Mason nodded. "Yeah...my *hero!*"

"Life will bring you challenges, but 90% of life is how you respond to them. Sometimes you'll succeed, and sometimes you'll fail, but both experiences will create memories that will stay with you until you find yourself at the pearly gates."

"You mean like Papa?"

"Yes, just like Papa! I've discovered that my biggest accomplishments have come after my biggest failures. Your challenging times become the bright spots in life that shape who you are and that define your character. It's in *those* moments that you need to take a deep breath, listen for your hero, and choose to respond in a way that you'll be *proud* to remember."

"Dad, I want to *believe* my hero, and I want to *be* the hero!"

"Remember, Mason, Daddy and Mommy love you very much!"

James gave Mason a kiss on the forehead and made an exaggerated sucking noise, trying to suck out all of Mason's bad dreams.

"I love you, Dad."

"I love you too, *Super Mason!*"

## TWENTY-FOUR

# Commitment Day
## Ready to Be the Hero?

James adjusted Mason's blanket and snuck out of his door, only to find Suzy standing there with tears rolling down her cheeks. "I never knew that Carl had so much impact on you," she said, sobbing. "You're back. The James I married is back!"

Suzy threw her arms around his neck, tilted her head ever so slightly to the left, and kissed him on the lips.

"Yeah, Suzy, life has thrown me some curve balls, but I wouldn't be the man I am today without them, and I wouldn't be the man I am today without you."

James squeezed Suzy tightly as they looked into each other's eyes.

"Suzy, I've been reminded about what matters most in life. I've been allowing the other voice to have too much influence on me lately. I know I need to pause and listen for my inner hero more often. Together there is no mountain too tall for us to climb and no challenge too massive for us to overcome."

"James, I'm so glad you said that. I know I've been kind of emotional lately, and I've been extra tough on you. Do you really think that we can overcome *anything* that comes our way?"

"Trust me, Suzy, nothing can come between us again. I'm grounded in my hero habits, and our family foundation is solid. I won't allow another perfect storm to churn our relationship, no matter how big and bad! I know that we are in control of our own destiny. I know what we *believe* drives our thoughts, our actions, and our reality.

"Never again, Suzy." James placed her hand on his heart. "*Never...*"

"But, James, sometimes we have little control over what's to come. It can feel like our world is crashing down around us. Sometimes it's easy to lose sight of the big picture. What about in *those* moments? What about when we climb the highest mountain and discover there are several more peaks?"

"Life is *simple*, but I've been overcomplicating it lately. I've been playing an unwinnable game, and I allowed my villain voice to start assuming negative intent. I was stressed and frustrated from trying to do it all myself, and that made it very easy to default to misery instead of *choosing happiness*.

Now that I've started asking for help and accepting feedback, *I'm playing a winnable game*. I know what winning looks like at work and at home. I'm open to humbling feedback that will help me stay on course. I know that *paying it forward* will give me more empathy so I can grant others the benefit of the doubt. It will keep me open to *assuming positive intent* when someone gifts me tough feedback that highlights my blind spots. We've realigned our schedules so we can get back to the gym and karate. We've renewed our Sunday-night calendaring ritual to *consult the owl* and evaluate our progress and direction instead of just skidding from one week into the next."

James paused, took a deep breath, looked deep into Suzy's eyes, and smiled.

"I know I need to do a better job of *being here* for you and Mason. I need to stay present and think through big decisions with you. I'm not perfect, and I know we will grow together through the challenges. I'll *choose happiness* so I can embrace the challenges, the successes, and all the moments in between. I know that I can choose to be happy in the toughest of times. *We* will be ready when the next perfect storm comes crashing in."

Suzy took a deep breath, threw her arms around James's shoulders, and allowed him to carry the weight of her world. James felt her whisper tickle the tiny hairs on his ear, giving him goosebumps.

"Recognition Man…I'm pregnant."

*Recognition Man*

The Journey Continues...

# The Invitation

James's story and struggle represents some aspect within each of us. When we push too hard for too long, we create distance from who we are intending to become. In those moments, it's easy to succumb to the sweet and enticing words of our inner villain.

This book is your leadership wake-up call, your opportunity to step back and evaluate if your thoughts, words and actions are drawing you closer to who you are and where you want to go.

I invite you to take a moment and consult your wise inner owl to determine which hero habit provides the most opportunity for improvement. Consider this your "time-out" before you rush back into the busyness of life to pause, reflect and grow.

*The Hero Habit I most need to focus on:*

DESIGN A WINNABLE GAME
ASSUME POSITIVE INTENT
CHOOSE HAPPINESS
BE ALL IN
BE HERE
PAY IT FORWARD
CONSULT THE OWL

# Hero Tribe

Congratulations and welcome to our hero habits tribe!
We are a group of overachievers who pushed too hard for too long and woke up one day in the midst of a perfect storm of challenges. We tried to overcome our circumstances by putting in long hours and sacrificing sleep, but when life overwhelmed us, we stumbled and our inner villain started to take control.

While your story from hero to villain and back to hero again might not seem that amazing to you, it could be the tipping point for someone who is struggling with their own perfect storm.

How you've transformed the *lead* in your life to *gold* could be the inspiration someone needs to reclaim their inner hero.
Please share your story and support others to *be the hero!*

*Discover more about your inner hero by visiting us at:*

## www.HeroHabits.org/MyHero

*How to be the hero in every situation...*

# Hero Habits

————

Hero Habit #1: **DESIGN A WINNABLE GAME**

Hero Habit #2: **ASSUME POSITIVE INTENT**

Hero Habit #3: **CHOOSE HAPPINESS**

Hero Habit #4: **BE ALL IN**

Hero Habit #5: **BE HERE**

Hero Habit #6: **PAY IT FORWARD**

Hero Habit #7: **CONSULT THE OWL**

*How to be the villain in every situation...*

# Villainous Vices

---

Villainous Vice #1: ACCEPT AN UNWINNABLE GAME

Villainous Vice #2: ASSUME NEGATIVE INTENT

Villainous Vice #3: DEFAULT TO MISERY

Villainous Vice #4: BE HALF IN

Villainous Vice #5: BE DISTRACTED

Villainous Vice #6: BE SELF-ABSORBED

Villainous Vice #7: BE RECKLESS

# Create a Hero Organization

## Keynote Speaking & Workshops

## **HERO HABITS**
The Seven Habits to Unleash the HERO in You

---

Are you struggling to keep up with the pace of change?

Is your organization experiencing growing pains that have caused unintended consequences?

Are you looking for something fun to boost teamwork and collaboration?

**If you answered yes to any of these questions, invite Michael to speak at your next event.**

Michael will engage your audience in a humorous deep dive, highlighting their leadership, communication, and problem-solving styles. His Hero versus Villain approach to leadership will INSPIRE your audience to BE THE HERO!

Michael Hahn will show you how to:

**Design a winnable game for yourself, team, and organization**

**Identify where hero strengths become villainous weaknesses**

**Assume positive intent in the face of pressure, deadlines, and stress**

**Learn real-life skills to lead your team from surviving to thriving**

———————

For speaking inquiries visit:

# www.MichaelHahnSpeaker.com

# Inspire a Hero Team

## Assessment & Coaching

## Why Coaching?

*Do you want to:*

Stop struggling to get your people to BE ALL IN?

Create a team culture that DRIVES business results?

Avoid the typical frustrations and pitfalls of leadership?

Hero Habits coaching enables you to SHIFT from being a good manager to become a GREAT leader!

During this six-month coaching program, you'll learn and practice effective strategies to expand your feedback, delegation, and accountability skills. You'll be assigned a hero habits coach to be your dedicated partner and to help you shift from surviving to *thriving* in business and in life.

The PREP personality assessment will be utilized to quickly understand your current situation and the specific challenges and opportunities inherent in your preferred personality style.

———

To evaluate options, visit:

# www.HeroHabits.org/Coaching

# If people don't think you're CRAZY, you're NOT thinking BIG enough!

— Hahndo

# Acknowledgments

This book was inspired by the real-life heroes I've encountered throughout my life. Your stories continue to inspire me to take the next step on this journey. Thank you.

First, I want to thank Jesus, my Lord and Savior, for giving me the patience, ability and faith required to write this book!

Thank you to Team Hahndo for your ongoing inspiration, encouragement, and support to bring Hero Habits to life.

Thank you to Bob Mallo, Leonard Collins, Stephanie Almeida, Maryse Gregoire, and all the Superstars. Your stories of personal alchemy inspired me to include specific portions within the book.

Thank you to Mike Hahn, Eric Schaefges, Steve Baker, Rich Diaz, Erin Peterson, Marshall Goldsmith, Barry Saltzman, and Keith McKinnon. Your feedback and coaching has created a richer and more impactful experience for our tribe.

A very special thank you to JoAn Mann, for your deep insights into personality dynamics, which have transformed my coaching and speaking. I look forward to continuing to learn from you!

Thank you to Carleen Jones, my mommy, who's always told me that I can do anything.

And thank you for reading this book and for taking the hero habits challenge to be the hero every day and in every way. It's not easy, but it's rewarding to discover who we were made to be.

Heroically,
**Michael Hahn a.k.a. Hahndo**

# About the Author

MICHAEL H. HAHN is an outstanding authority and international speaker on organizational culture, employee engagement, and personal mastery. He speaks to audiences across North America at conferences, sales kickoffs, and corporate events.

Michael's massive impact at Allstate insurance and other high-growth organizations has been attributed to his grassroots approach to engaging employees in the culture movement.

His ACES model and his *Culture Change Handbook* have been featured in dozens of articles and publications for a variety of organizations and associations. In 2015, he won the Public Relations Society of America Award for Brand Management and Reputation for his leadership of the Allstate Ambassador culture movement.

Michael holds a dual MBA in entrepreneurship & leadership and change management from DePaul University and a BS in finance from Northern Illinois University. He has twenty-plus years of corporate experience in finance, strategy, business development, HR, and corporate relations.

For speaking, coaching and consulting
inquiries, e-mail **Info@MichaelHahnSpeaker.com**